Phil Myers
11/(...)

THE Hidden Life of Prayer

The Hidden Life of Prayer

DAVID M'INTYRE

BETHANY HOUSE PUBLISHERS
MINNEAPOLIS, MINNESOTA 55438

Published by Bethany House Publishers
A Ministry of Bethany Fellowship, Inc.
11300 Hampshire Avenue South,
Minneapolis, Minnesota 55438

Printed in the United States of America

Library of Congress Cataloging-in-Publication Data

M'Intyre, David M., 1859–1938.
The hidden life of prayer / David M. M'Intyre
p. cm.
1. Prayer—Christianity. I. Title.
BV215.M15 1993
248.3'2—dc20 93-24298
ISBN 1-55661-365-2 CIP

Contents

Biography of David M. M'Intyre, D.D.

by Rev. Professor Francis Davidson, D.D.

It is fitting that a brief prologue should accompany this edition of *The Hidden Life of Prayer*, for the saintly author has since received his coronation.

Preeminently, David Martin M'Intyre was a man of prayer. He lived in the presence of God. It is a major mistake, however, to imagine that he was "so heavenly as to be no earthly good." He was a practical mystic. Like Moses, he descended the mount of communion with God, his face shining, and in the divine power became a great leader of multitudes.

His Birth and Re-birth

The author of this and many other books was a son of the manse, born at Monikie, Angus, in 1859. Of those early years he speaks of himself: "I was brought up in a Christian home—an ordinary child, with an adequate sense of what was fitting, and no grave delinquencies. I had not 'broken the fold of God.' Yet I was often painfully aware that I had not entered the Kingdom of the Divine Love."

He soon experienced the quest for God which, in later years, was revealed as God's quest for him. But meantime, the goal was not long distant, for soon a familiar text went through his mind like a ray of light: "Believe on the Lord Jesus Christ and thou shalt be saved." The tender heart of a lad was then irrevocably yielded to the Lord: "Immediately, without an instant's delay, I rested my soul on Christ, and was at peace. Since that time I have never doubted that my Lord has undertaken on my behalf. There was very little difference in my outward life after this; but the inward change was very great. Now I began to rejoice in God my Savior, and I have never lost the comfort of that good hour. Though I mourn when I recall the disappointments with which I must often have touched the heart of the Redeemer, yet during almost the space of a lifetime, God has been the 'gladness of my joy,' and I trust I shall come to the Eternal Summer with the Springtime of my first love unspent."

His Early Years

His academic career centered in Edinburgh, and while still a student he was invited to be a missionary in St. John's Church, Leith, under the guidance of Dr. Kelman, father of the famous minister of St. George's Church, Edinburgh. He had brief experiences in various places thereafter—Dundee, Willesden, and Drury Lane, London—till he was placed in charge of an English Presbyterian Extension Church in College Park, Kensal Rise, London. Two years of earnest labor passed quickly, and the eager student returned to Edinburgh to complete his theological curriculum. That growing church never forgot their young missionary. During his course in Edinburgh, the Presbytery of London had raised the station at College Park to the full status of a pastoral charge. At once the congregation called him. It was not the licentiate's ideal.

His dream was of a country parish, but his destiny was otherwise ordered. The deputation that met him moved him mightily: "We are a band of men whose hearts the Lord has touched." So David M. M'Intyre launched out on his career and was ordained at College Park Church, London, in 1886.

His Ministry

For five full years he remained in London till, in 1891, he was called to become colleague and successor to the saintly Dr. Andrew A. Bonar, then in the zenith of his influence. Finnieston Church was the home of evangelism, and because of its echoing chord in his heart, the apprentice minister dared to accept the invitation, being borne on by the force of circumstances and the all-wise providence of God, the very God to whom he had unreservedly committed his whole life. The partnership lasted only some fifteen months, for it was severed by the passing of the senior minister; but life is not measured by time. Deep were the impressions made on the mind and spirit of the younger man in that brief period. Left as sole shepherd of a distinguished flock, he essayed to follow in the hallowed footsteps of his beloved colleague.

Nearly two years after the lamented death of Andrew A. Bonar, David M. M'Intyre married Jane Christian Bonar, the third daughter of his late senior colleague. It was a happy union. At his jubilee, and in her hearing, his loving tribute was, "To myself she has been as an angel of God." She shared his long life to the end, and lived after him for about two years.

As sole minister of Finnieston, he developed into an ideal pastor and a preacher of some note. He never was a sparkling orator or popular star. Indeed, he never attempted such flights. His values were elsewhere. His fort lay in the devotional exposition of the living Word. His springs were ever fresh and deep. His delivery was quiet and even in tone, but the sincerity of both mind and spirit was unmistakable. He shot his well-polished shaft home, where many a more ornate preacher failed. This Finnieston ministry, greatly blessed of God, lasted from 1891 to 1914, when he became minister emeritus with his delightful colleague, the Rev. William Simpson, M.A.

Principal of the Glasgow Bible Training Institute

In 1913, while still minister of Finnieston, Dr. M'Intyre accepted the invitation of the Directors of the Glasgow Bible Training Institute to succeed Mr. John Anderson as principal. It was found impossible to carry on the two spheres efficiently, and in 1915 he was content to become honorary senior minister of Finnieston, and to devote all his energies to the training of students for the home and foreign fields. This work he nobly discharged. During his tenure as principal, over one thousand students passed through the college, the majority of whom were destined for foreign mission fields.

I came into contact with Dr. M'Intyre when I was invited by him to become a visiting lecturer on biblical and systematic theology, some five years before I succeeded him in the supreme direction of the curriculum. He was an ideal chief of staff. The impression made on his colleagues was always how much he was indebted to them for their assistance. Seldom did he give any of us the chance to feel how much we owed to him. He liked a cup of tea at eleven, and on my lecture days he would have me join him. Then it was that his quiet humor could be seen. Of all men he was most sympathetic. Very often his phrase was, "I am sorry about that." His students loved him. He cared for them all as a father. He may have spoiled them, but one had to admire his extreme generosity, even defend it.

His Jubilee

The ministerial Jubilee of the Rev. David M. M'Intyre, D.D., was celebrated in Finnieston Church in May 1936. It was a great occasion. The atmosphere was charged with joy and thanksgiving. Friends from all parts gathered to honor him, to whom verily honor was due. The Right Honorable Lord Maclay, P.C., LL.D., J.P., in the name of the assembly, seen and unseen, made the presentation of a check for £500. The congregation gave a plaque, modestly designed and tooled in gold, a passage of which is the following:

> We rejoice to know that the influence of your ministry has extended far beyond the bounds of your beloved Finnieston. You are highly esteemed in all the churches as an Evangelist approved of God, as a scholar and theologian skilled in the deep things of God, as an organizer of prayer circles among the people of God, and as a writer, whose helpful books have attained a wide circulation, in recognition of which to our great pride and gratification, the Senate of Glasgow conferred upon you the degree of Doctor of Divinity.

Many were the tributes paid that evening, and in reply the humble recipient made a memorable speech, revealing much of his life and character hitherto both known and unknown. He was unstinted in the praise of others. His closing words were most moving: "My ministry must now be nearing its close. I have entered that region which lies along the frontier of the King's country, where, as John Bunyan tells us, the contrast between the Bride and the Bridegroom is ofttimes renewed. It is the covenant of free grace: not by works of righteousness which we have done, but according to His mercy He saved us. On His word, and on His completed work, I rest."

The Man

Dr. M'Intyre passed into glory on March 8, 1938. The messenger who summoned him had for some time been drawing near. The doctor became obviously frail and subject to severe attacks of bronchitis. Yet he manfully gripped the reins and guided his affairs to the very end. He wished to die in harness.

The only time I ever saw his placid nature agitated was once when he was threatened to be relieved of all his work, and begged to consider his retirement. He was wedded to his work. An indefatigable toiler was perhaps the first characteristic of the man to be observed. The absurdity of the case was obvious when he would caution others to be careful and take more rest!

His parish was the Bible, and he walked its length and breadth with reverent and scholarly stride. A master of detail, he was gifted with the analytical mind more than the synthetical. He had rare spiritual insight and an almost uncanny power of discerning character. Yet he was not supremely a man of affairs, a businessman; for while not inefficient, his values lay elsewhere than in this world.

He was no ecclesiastic, although a loyal churchman. A fearless theologian, the doctor was staunch in his support of the evangelical fundamentals, yet not by any means an obscurantist. He was a progressive conservative in doctrine and no partisan to any labels of theology. His particular school was the comprehensive New Testament. It need not be here recorded that David M. M'Intyre was conspicuously a man of prayer. He walked and talked with God. As a writer he was voluminous. Himself a wide reader, he was essentially a book-lover, and his contribution to biblical and devotional literature is still greatly prized. Apart from the living epistles on which he wrote extensively, in many lands today, Dr. M'Intyre's numerous books keep his name alive and impress his mystic mind upon thousands of grateful readers.

Preface

The occasion that has prompted the dedication of this book permits me to inscribe upon it the honored name of Dr. Andrew A. Bonar, and to recall the fervent devotion which characterized those who were most intimately associated with him in the service of Christ.

The Diary of Dr. Bonar, already a Christian classic, is probably the best treatise on private prayer that we possess. Originally meant to mark the memorabilia of his life, it became, almost exclusively, an instrument for recording and testing his prayers.

On Thursday, December 4, 1856, Mr. Bonar was inducted into the pastoral charge of Finnieston Church, Glasgow. On the evening of that day he signified anew his sense of the value of prayer: "The Lord filled me with desire, and made me feel that I must be as much with Him alone as with souls in public."

A few months later he wrote, "For nearly ten days I have been much hindered in prayer, and feel my strength weakened thereby. I must at once return, through the Lord's strength, to not less than three hours a day spent in prayer and meditation upon the Word."

On the first anniversary of this entry he wrote, "Tomorrow I propose to spend most of the day in prayer in the Church. Lord, help me." Later, we find him setting apart one whole day in each month for prayer and fasting. But his devotion overflowed all prepared channels. The following sentences carry with them their own instruction: "I felt in the evening most bitter grief over the apathy of the district. They are perishing! They are perishing! Yet they will not consider. I lay awake, thinking over, and crying to the Lord in broken groans."

Again, he observes, "I should count the days, not by what I have of new instances of usefulness, but by the times I have been enabled to pray in faith, and to take hold upon God." At another time he remarks that "prayer should make room for itself"; again, that it should "interweave" itself into all work for Christ; that in "the incessant occupations, the bustle of even right things, Satan may find his opportunity to hinder prayer." He quotes Flavel: "The devil is aware that one hour of close fellowship, hearty converse with God in prayer, is able to pull down what he has been contriving and building many a year." He adds from his own experience: "Satan, like the lapwing, drew me away from the real object (prayer and fellowship with God) by suggesting every now and then something about some other part of my work . . . and so the best hours of yesterday were in a great measure lost, so far as 'prayer and transfiguration' might have been."

His holidays were special opportunities for "trading with the talent of prayer." "I see," he writes, "that the Master teaches as much the necessity of such times of continued waiting on God as a stay in the country." In sailing to America to attend the Northfield Conference, and in returning, he was "enabled to pray some hours every day on the ship." Of his frequent visits to Mull, he writes, "The best thing I have found in this quiet island has been seasons of prayer."

As he reviewed his ministry from time to time, amid many regrets his deepest sorrow was the unexhausted possibilities of prayer: "My heart smites me still for not being like Epaphras, who 'is always wrestling in prayer' (Colossians 4:12). . . . One terrible failure confronted me everywhere, 'You have not asked for anything in my name' (John 16:24). . . . Lack of prayer in right measure and manner . . . Had an almost overwhelming sense of sins of omission in the days past. If only I had prayed more. . . . Oh, that I had prayed a hundredfold more."

Perhaps the most intimate of Dr. Bonar's ministerial associates was Robert Murray M'Cheyne. His prayerfulness has almost become a proverb. Dr. James Hamilton writes of him, "He gave himself to prayer. Like his blessed Master, he often rose up a great while before it was day, and spent the time in singing psalms and hymns and the devotional reading of that Word which dwelt so richly in him. His walks, rides, and journeys were sanctified by prayer. . . . There was nothing he liked so much as to go out into a solitary place and pray; and the ruined chapel of Invergowrie, and many other sequestered spots around Dundee, were the much-loved resorts where he had often enjoyed sweet communion with God.

"Seldom have we known one so specific and yet reverential in his prayers, nor one whose confessions of sin united such self-loathing with such filial love. Now that 'Moses my servant is dead,' perhaps the heaviest loss to his brethren, his people, and the land, is the loss of his intercession."

Only a few months before his death, Mr. M'Cheyne drew up some considerations touching "Reformation in Secret Prayer."

"I ought," he said, "to spend the best hours of the day in communion with God. It is my noblest and most fruitful employment, and is not to be thrust into any corner." This paper on personal reformation was evidently left unfinished. "And now," adds his biographer, "he knows even as he is known."

Dr. Moody Stuart was a friend greatly beloved. Of him his biographer writes, "Dr. Moody Stuart was preeminently a man of prayer. . . . He prayed without ceasing. . . . He prayed always, with all prayer and supplication in the Spirit, watching with all perseverance. He felt that nothing was too small for him to bring to his God in prayer, and that nothing was too great for him to ask in Jesus' name. . . . Prayer was to him second nature."

His own testimony was, "I cannot say that a day passes without beholding the beauty of the Lord, and being revived by His grace. For the most part, the Lord is with me the greater part of the day, and is daily giving me some new insight into the depth and freedom of His love, together with the conviction of sin and contrition of spirit, in which there is much peace and rest." The rules that he offered to others, and in accordance with which he guided his own prayer life, were (1) Pray till you pray; (2) Pray till you are conscious of being heard; (3) Pray till you receive an answer.

Dr. A. N. Somerville was another "true yokefellow." In the work of his own congregation, it was his custom "to go into the church alone, and read the names on the pews, committing each member to God in prayer." When the missionary hunger seized and held his heart, he spread open before him an atlas, and prayed for men of every nation and kindred and people and tongue. From the chair of the general assembly of his church, he exhorted her members to address themselves to more fervent and believing intercession. "The greatest, most successful servants Christ ever had have divided their functions into two departments: 'We will give ourselves continually to prayer and to the ministry of the Word.' What would be thought of dividing the twelve hours of our day by giving six hours to prayer for the Gospel, and six to the ministry of the Word? Had all Christ's servants acted thus, could anyone estimate how mighty the results on the world would be today?"

It is said of William C. Burns, another fellow-soldier, "His whole life was literally a life of prayer. His whole ministry a series of battles fought at the mercy seat." Very early in his ministerial course he gave it as his judgment that "The great, fundamental error, as far as I can see, in the economy of the Christian life, which many, and alas, I for one commit, is that of having too few and too short periods of solemn retirement with our gracious Father and His loving Son, Jesus Christ." From this opinion he never swerved. He spent days and sometimes nights "before the Lord," and sighed, "Oh, for a day every week to spend entirely in the secret of His presence." For weeks before the Kilsyth awakening, as his brother informs us, "he was full of prayer. He seemed to care for nothing but to pray. In the daytime, alone, or with others, it was his chief delight, and in the night watches he might be heard praying aloud." The Lord whom he sought came to His temple suddenly.

One might speak of John Milne of Perth, Patrick Miller of Dundee, Daniel Cormick of Kirriemuir, Dr. Bonar's brothers, Dr. James Hamilton of London, Joseph Wilson of Abernyte, and the rest, their "friends and companions." Let it suffice to mention only one other, William Hewitson of Dirleton. Dr. A. Bonar says of him, "One thing often struck me in Mr. Hewitson. He seemed to have no intervals in communion with God—no gaps. I used to feel, when with him, that it was being with one who was a vine watered every moment." So it was that he was able to say with truth, "I am better acquainted with Jesus than with any friend I have on earth."

Books on secret prayer are without number, but it seems to me that there is still room for one in which an appeal may be taken, steadily, and from every point, to life—to the experience of God's saints. In these pages no attempt has been made to explain the mysteries of communion with God and commerce with heaven. What is here offered is a simple enumeration of some things that the Lord's remembrancers have found to be helpful in the practice of prayer. The great Bengel explained that if he desired the most perfect intimacy with real Christians on one account rather than another, it was "for the sake of learning how they manage in secret to keep up their communion with God."

Lord, teach us to pray.

My God, Thy creature answer Thee.

—*Alfred de Musset*

The love of Christ is my prayer book.

—*Gerhard Tersteegen*

Prayer is the key of heaven; the Spirit helps faith to turn this key.

—*Thomas Watson*

1

The Life of Prayer

In one of the cathedrals of Northern Europe an exquisite group in high relief represents the prayer life. It is arrayed in three panels. The first of these reminds us of the apostolic decree, "Pray without ceasing." We see the front of a spacious temple that opens onto the marketplace. The great square is strewn with knots of eager men, gesticulating, haggling, bargaining—all evidently intent on profit. But One, who wears a circlet of thorns, and is clothed in a garment woven without seam from the top throughout, moves silently through the clamorous crowds and subdues to holy fear the most covetous heart.

The second panel displays the precincts of the temple, and serves to illustrate the common worship of the Church. White-robed ministrants scurry in every direction. They carry oil for the lamp, water for the washing basin, and blood from the altar. They are filled with pure intentions, and their eyes are turned toward the unseen glory while they fulfill the duties of their sacred calling.

The third panel introduces to us the inner sanctuary. A solitary worshiper has entered within the veil. Hushed and lowly in the presence of God, he bends before the glancing

Shekinah. This represents the hidden life of prayer of which the Master spoke in the familiar words, "When you pray, go into your room, close the door and pray to your Father, who is unseen. Then your Father, who sees what is done in secret, will reward you" (Matthew 6:6).

Our Lord takes it for granted that His people will pray. Indeed, in Scripture the outward obligation of prayer is implied rather than asserted. Moved by a divinely implanted instinct, our natures cry out for God, for the living God. This instinct may be crushed in many different ways by sin, and yet it awakens with power when confronted by the weight of redemption. Christians of every type and theologians of all schools agree in their recognition of this principle of the new life. Chrysostom has said, "The just man does not desist from praying until he ceases to be just." Augustine declared, "He that loves little prays little, and he that loves much prays much." Richard Hooker wrote, "Prayer is the first thing with which a righteous life begins, and the last with which it ends." Pére la Combe said, "He who has a pure heart will never cease to pray, and he who will be constant in prayer shall know what it is to have a pure heart." John Bunyan proclaimed, "If you are not a praying person, you are not a Christian." Richard Baxter called prayer "the breath of the new creature," and George Herbert called it "the soul's blood."

Difficulty in Prayer

Despite our instinctive dependence upon God, no duty is more earnestly impressed upon us in Scripture than the duty of continual communication with Him. The main reason for this unceasing insistence is the difficulty of prayer. In its nature it is a laborious undertaking. In our attempts to maintain the spirit of prayer we are called to wrestle against principalities and the powers of darkness.

"Dear Christian reader," says Jacob Boehme, "to pray properly is rigorous work." Prayer is the most sublime energy of which the spirit of man is capable.

> Believe me, to pray with all your heart and strength, with the reason and the will, to believe vividly that God will listen to your voice through Christ, and, indeed, to do the thing He pleases immediately following that—this is the last, the greatest achievement of the Christian's warfare upon earth. Teach us to pray, O Lord.
>
> —Coleridge

It is in one aspect glory and blessedness. In another it is drudgery and distress, battle and agony. Uplifted hands begin to quiver long before the field is won. Straining sinews and panting breath proclaim the exhaustion of the "heavenly footman." The weight that falls upon an aching heart bedews the brow with anguish, even when the midnight air is chill. Prayer is the elevation of the earth-bound soul into the heavens, the entrance of the purified spirit into the holiest. It is the rending of the luminous veil that shuts in, as if behind curtains, the glory of God. Prayer is the vision of things unseen, the recognition of the mind of the Spirit, the effort to frame words which man may not utter.

"A man that truly prays one prayer," says Bunyan, "shall after that never be able to express with his mouth or pen the unutterable desires, sense, affection, and longing that went to God in that prayer." The saints of the early church had an insatiable energy in intercession. "Battering the gates of heaven with storms of prayer," they took the kingdom of heaven by violence. The first Christians proved, in the wilderness, in the dungeon, in the arena, and at the stake, the truth of their Master's words, "My Father will give you whatever you ask in my name" (John 16:23).

Their souls ascended to God in supplication as the flame of the altar mounts heavenward. The orthodox Jews in their Talmud affirm that in the divine life four things call for fortitude and one of these is prayer. Someone who met Tersteegen at Kronenberg remarked, "It seemed to me as if he had gone straight into heaven and had lost himself in God. When he was done praying he was often as white as the wall." David Brainerd notes that on one occasion he found his soul "exceedingly enlarged" in supplication. He was "in such anguish, and pleaded with so much earnestness and importunity" that when he rose from his knees he felt "extremely weak and overcome." "I could scarcely walk straight," he goes on to say, "my joints were loosed, the sweat ran down my face and body, and nature seemed as if it would dissolve." Dr. Horton, in Verbum Dei, reminded us of John Foster, who used to spend long nights in his chapel, absorbed in spiritual exercises. He went pacing to and fro with an uneasiness in his spirit, until his restless feet had worn a little track in the aisle.

One might easily multiply examples, but there is no need to go beyond Scripture to find either precept or example to impress us with the difficulty of prayer that prevails. Hear the supplication of the psalmist, "Preserve my life according to your word . . . preserve my life in your righteousness . . . preserve my life according to your love . . . preserve my life, O Lord, according to your laws. . . . For your name's sake, O Lord, preserve my life" (Psalm 119:25, 40, 88, 149; 143:11). Listen to the complaint of the prophet, "No one calls on your name or strives to lay hold of you" (Isaiah 64:7).

Should not their cries find an echo in our experience? Do we know what it is to "labor," to "wrestle," to "agonize" in prayer? Martin Luther wrote that "it is a tremendously hard thing to pray properly. It is the science of all sciences to pray so that the heart may approach God, with all gracious confidence, and say, 'Our Father, which art in heaven.' For whoever has such confidence of grace is already over the hill called Difficulty, and has laid the foundation-stone of the temple of prayer." Catherine of Siena declared, "Perfect prayer is not attained by the use of many words, but through deep desire."

Another explanation of the difficulty of prayer lies in the fact that we are spiritually hindered. Paul assures us that we shall have to maintain our prayer energy "against the powers of this dark world and against the spiritual forces of evil in the heavenly realms" (Ephesians 6:12). Dr. Andrew Bonar used to say that as the King of Aram commanded his captains not to fight anyone small or great, but only with the king of Israel (1 Kings 22:31), so the prince of the power of the air seems to bend all the force of his attack against the spirit of prayer. If he should prove victorious there, he has won the day.

"When we go to God by prayer, the devil knows we gain strength against him, and therefore he opposes us all he can" (R. Sibbes). Sometimes we are conscious of a satanic impulse directed immediately against the life of prayer in our souls. Sometimes we are led into the parched misery of the wilderness experience, and the face of God grows dark above us. Sometimes when we strive most earnestly to bring every thought and imagination under obedience to Christ, we seem to succumb to disorder and unrest. Sometimes the inbred laziness of our nature lends itself to the evil one as an instrument by which he turns our minds away from the exercise of prayer.

John Climacus said that "we know the effectiveness of prayer by the efforts of the wicked spirits to distract us during the divine office. We experience the fruit of prayer in the defeat of our enemies." Because of all these things, therefore, we must be diligent and resolved. We must watch as if we were a sentry who understands that the lives of men are dependent on our wakefulness, resourcefulness, and courage. "What I say to you," said the Lord to His disciples, "I say to everyone: 'Watch!' " (Mark 13:37).

Weakness in Prayer

There are times when even the soldiers of Christ become careless of their trust, and no longer guard with vigilance the gift of prayer. If you find a weariness in this duty, suspect yourself. Purge and purify your heart from the love of all sin, and try to put it into a heavenly and spiritual frame. Then you will find that prayer is not an unpleasant exercise, but is full of delight and satisfaction. Do not complain of the hardness of the duty, but of the contrary nature of your own heart. Should anyone who reads these pages be conscious of loss of power in intercession, lack of joy in communion, or hardness of heart in confession, "Remember the height from which you have fallen! Repent and do the things you did at first" (Revelation 2:5).

Oh, stars of heaven that fade and flame,
Oh, whispering waves below!
Was earth, or heaven, or I the same,
A year, a year ago!
The stars have kept their home on high,
The waves their wonted flow;
The love is lost that once was mine,
A year, a year ago.

—F. W.H. Myers

The only remedy for this languid mood is that we should "rekindle our love," as Polycarp wrote to the Church in Ephesus, "in the blood of God." Let us ask for a fresh gift of the Holy Spirit to quicken our sluggish hearts, a new disclosure of the charity of God. The Spirit will help our frailties, and the compassion of the Son of God will fall upon us. It will cloth us with zeal as with a garment, stirring our emotions into a most vehement flame, and filling our souls with heaven.

"[People] should always pray"—although a feebleness of spirit accompanies prayer like a shadow—"and not give up" (Luke 18:1). The soil in which the prayer of faith takes root is a life of unbroken communion with God, a life in which the windows of the soul are always open toward the City of Rest. We do not know the true potency of prayer until our hearts are so intently fixed on God that our thoughts turn to Him whenever they are set free from the consideration of earthly things. Origen said that his life was "one unceasing supplication." It is by this principle above all others that the perfect idea of the Christian life is realized.

Continuous Prayer

On October 7, 1860, Andrew Bonar wrote in his diary: "I see that unless I keep up short prayer at intervals, every day throughout the whole day, I lose the spirit of prayer. I would never lose sight at any time of the Lamb in the midst of the throne, and if I have this sight I shall be able to pray."

The great Princeton scholar Jonathan Edwards said, "My mind was greatly fixed on divine things: almost perpetually in the contemplation of them. I spent most of my time in thinking of divine things, year after year; often walking alone in the woods and solitary places, for meditation, soliloquy, prayer, and converse with God; and it was always my manner to sing forth my contemplations. . . . Prayer seemed to be natural to me, as the breath by which the inward burnings of my heart had vent" (*Memoirs*, ch. 1). "In our mutual conversation—amid all the busiest scenes of our pilgrimage—we may be moving to and fro on the rapid wing of prayer.

Mental prayer—that prayer that lays the whole burden of the heart on a single sigh. A sigh breathed in the spirit, though inaudible to all around us but God, may sanctify every conversation, every event in the history of the day. We must have fellowship at all times either with the spirit of the world or with the Spirit of God.

"Prayer will be fatiguing to both flesh and blood if uttered aloud and sustained long. Oral prayer and prayer mentally ordered in words though not spoken cannot be engaged in without ceasing. Instead there is an undercurrent of prayer that may run continually under the stream of our thoughts and never weary us. Such prayer is the silent breathing of the Spirit of God who dwells in our hearts (see Romans 8:9 and 1 Corinthians 3:16). It is the temper and habit of the spiritual mind; it is the pulse of our life which is hid with Christ in God" (Hewitson's *Life*, pp. 100, 101).

"The vision of God," says Bishop Westcott, "makes life a continuous prayer." In that vision all fleeting things resolve themselves, and appear in relation to things unseen. In a broad use of the term, prayer is the sum of all the service that we render to God. All fulfillment of this duty is, in one sense, the performance of divine service, and the familiar saying, "Work is worship," is justified. "I am a man of prayer," said the psalmist (Psalm 109:4). "In everything, by prayer and petition, with thanksgiving," said an apostle (Philippians 4:6).

In the Old Testament, the life that is steeped in prayer is often described as a walk with God. Enoch walked in assurance, Abraham in perfection, Elijah in truth, the sons of Levi in peace and equity. Many times it is spoken of as a dwelling with God, even as Joshua departed not from the Tabernacle; or as certain craftsmen of old lived with a king for his work. Again, it is defined as the ascent of the soul into the Sacred Presence; as the planets reflect the Lord's glory, climbing into the light of the sun's countenance; or as a flower, lit with beauty and dipped in fragrance, reaches upward toward the light. At other times, prayer is said to be the gathering up of all the senses in an ardor of reverence, love, and praise. As one clear strain may succeed in reducing to harmony a number of mutually discordant voices, so the dominant impulses of the spiritual nature unite the heart to fear the name of the Lord.

The most familiar, and perhaps the most impressive description of prayer in the Old Testament, is found in those numerous passages where the life of communion with God is spoken of as waiting upon Him. The great scholar A. B. Davidson has given a beautiful definition of waiting upon God: "To wait is not merely to remain impassive. It is to expect—to look for with patience, and also with submission. It is to long for, but not impatiently; to look for, but not to fret at the delay; to watch for, but not restlessly; to feel that if He does not come we will acquiesce, and yet to refuse to let the mind acquiesce in the feeling that He will not come."

Now, do not let anyone say that such a life is idealistic and serves no purpose. The real world is not a covering veil of reason and sensibility. Reality belongs to those heavenly things of which the earthly are mere patterns and conformities. Who is so practical as God? Who among us has so wisely directed their efforts to the circumstances and occasions they were called to face as "the Son of Man who is in heaven"? Those who pray well, work well. Those who pray most, achieve the grandest results. As Tauler said in a striking phrase, "In God nothing is hindered."

Habitual Prayer

The cultivation of the habit of prayer will secure its expression on all suitable occasions. In times of need almost everyone will pray. Moses stood on the shores of the Red Sea, surveying the panic of the children of Israel when they realized that the chariots of Pharaoh were thundering down upon them. "Why are you crying out to me?" said the Lord to Moses (Exodus 14:15). Nehemiah stood before King Artaxerxes. The monarch noticed the prophet's inward grief, and said, "Why does your face look so sad when you are not ill? This can be nothing but sadness of heart" (Nehemiah 2:2). That question opened the door to admit the answer to three months of praying. The hot desire that had risen to God in those slow months gathered itself into one fervent outcry, "Then I prayed to the God of heaven" (Nehemiah 2:4).

One whose life is spent in fellowship with God will constantly seek and find opportunities for swift and frequent approaches to the throne of grace. The apostles brought every duty under the cross. At the name of Jesus their loyal souls soared heavenward in adoration and in praise. The early Christians never met without invoking a benediction; they never parted without prayer. The saints of the Middle Ages allowed each passing incident to summon them to intercession—the shadow on the dial, the church bell, the flight of the swallow, the rising of the sun, the falling of a leaf.

The covenant that Sir Thomas Browne made with himself is well known: "To pray in all places where quietness invites—in any house, highway, or street. To know no street in this city that may not witness that I have not forgotten God and my Savior in it. That no parish or town where I have been may not say the like. To take occasion of praying upon the sight of any church I see or pass by as I ride about. To pray daily, and particularly for my sick patients and for all sick people no matter whose care they are under. At the entrance into the house of the sick to say, 'The peace and the mercy of God be upon this house.' After a sermon to make a prayer and desire a blessing, and to pray for the minister."

Once more, one who lives in the spirit of prayer will spend much time in retired and intimate communion with God. It is by such a deliberate engagement of prayer that the fresh springs of devotion that flow through the day are fed. Even though communion with God is the life-energy of the rewarded nature, our souls cleave to the dust (Psalm 119:25, KJV). Devotion tends to grow formal and becomes emptied of its spiritual content, exhausting itself in outward acts. The Master reminds us of this grave peril and informs us that the true defense against insincerity in our approach to God lies in the diligent exercise of private prayer. "Whoever is diligent in public prayers, and yet negligent in private, it is feared seek to approve themselves to men rather than to God" (*The Whole Duty of Man*, p. 119).

In the days of the Commonwealth, one of the early Quakers, "a servant of the Lord, but a stranger outwardly," came into an assembly of serious people who had met for worship. "After some time of waiting on the Lord in spirit, he had an opportunity to speak. All became silent. He said by way of exhortation, 'Keep to the Lord's watch.' These words, being spoken in the power of God had its active influence upon most of the meeting. Some felt great dread and fear upon their spirits. . . . After a little time he spoke again, saying, 'What I say to you, I say to all. Watch.' Then he was silent again a little time, but the whole meeting, being sensible that this man was under some extraordinary spirit and power, were all pondering what manner of teaching this should be. His was such a voice that most of the hearers had never heard before. It carried such great authority with it that it was unavoidable for them to be subject to the power" (Harvey, *The Rise of the Quakers*, pp. 73-74).

Soldier of Christ, you are in an enemy country; "Keep to the Lord's watch."

Remember that in the Levitical Law there is a frequent commemoration and charge given of the two daily sacrifices, the one to offer up in the morning and the other in the evening. These offerings by incense our holy, harmless, and undefiled High Priest has taken away, and instead of them, every devout Christian is at the appointed times to offer up a spiritual sacrifice, namely, that of prayer: for 'God is a Spirit, and they that worship Him must worship Him in spirit and in truth.' At these prescribed times, if you will have your prayers ascend up before God, you must withdraw from all outward occupations, to prepare for the inward and divine.

—Henry Vaughan, Silurist

God comes to me in silent hours,
As morning dew to summer flowers.

—Mechthild von Magdeburg

It will never be altogether well with us till we convert the universe into a prayer room, and continue in the Spirit as we go from place to place. . . . The prayer hour is left standing before God till the other hours come and stand beside it; then, if they are found to be a harmonious sisterhood, the prayer is granted.

—George Bowen

2
The Equipment

"When you pray, go into your room, close the door and pray to your Father" (Matthew 6:6). "Concerning this type of prayer," says Walter Hilton of Thurgarton in his *Scale of Perfection*. "Our Lord spoke figuratively: 'The fire on the altar must be kept burning; it must not go out. Every morning the priest is to add firewood and arrange the burnt offering on the fire' (Leviticus 6:12). That is, the fire of love shall forever be lighted in the soul of a devout and clean man or woman, which is God's altar. Every morning the priest is to lay sticks, and nourish the fire; that is, this person shall by holy psalms, clean thoughts, and fervent desire, nourish the fire of love in their heart, that it may not go out at any time." The equipment for the inner life of prayer is simple if not always easily obtained. It consists particularly of a quiet place, a quiet hour, and a quiet heart.

The Quiet Place

The first of these pieces of equipment is well within our reach. However, there are tens of thousands of our fellow believers who find it generally impossible to withdraw into the desired seclusion of the secret place. A mother at home in a crowded tenement, an apprentice in city lodgings, a farm laborer in his hut, a soldier in barracks, a student living at school, these and many more may not always to be able to command quiet and solitude. But remember that "your Father knows" (Matthew 6:8). It is comforting to reflect that the very Prince of the pilgrims shared the experience of such as these. In the carpenter's cottage in Nazareth there were, it appears, no fewer than nine persons who lived under one roof. There was the Holy Child, Mary His mother, and Joseph. There were also the Lord's brothers—four of them—and at least two sisters. Let us suppose that their home consisted principally of a living room, the workshop, and an inner chamber (a store closet where the provisions for the day, the kitchen utensils, the firewood, were laid). That gloomy recess had a latch on the inner side, placed there, it may be, by the carpenter's Son. That dark chamber was His private place, no less sacred than the cloud-wrapped shrine of the Presence in the Temple.

The late Dr. John Paton, of the New Hebrides, tells of such a prayer chamber in his father's modest dwelling:

> Our home consisted of a kitchen, a living room and a mid-room—or chamber—called the "closet." The closet was a very small compartment between the other two, having room only for a bed, a little table, and a chair, with a diminutive window shedding an extremely small amount of light on the scene. This was the sanctuary of that cottage home. Daily, and many times during the day, generally after each meal, we saw our father retire, and shut the door. We children got to understand, by a sort of spiritual instinct (for the thing was too sacred to be talked about), that prayers were being poured out there for us, just as in the days of old by the High Priest within the veil in the Most Holy Place. We occasionally

heard the pathetic echoes of a trembling voice, pleading as if for life. We learned to slip in and out past that door on tiptoe, so as not to disturb the holy colloquy. The outside world might not know, but we knew whence came that happy light, like that of a newborn smile, that always was dawning on my father's face. It was a reflection from the divine Presence, in the consciousness of which he lived. Never, in temple or cathedral, in mountain or glen, can I hope to feel the Lord God more near, more visibly walking and talking with men, than He did under that humble cottage roof of thatch and oak framework (Dr. John G. Paton, *Autobiography*, pp. 10–11).

After our Lord had entered His public ministry, there were occasions when He found it difficult to secure the privilege of solitude. He frequently received hospitality from those who showed Him the scantiest of courtesy and offered Him no facility for seclusion. When His spirit hungered for communion with His Father, He was glad to bend His steps toward the rough uplands:

Cold mountains and the midnight air
Witnessed the fervor of His prayer.

When He came up to Jerusalem for the Feasts, He was a homeless man. It was His custom to resort to the olive garden of Gethsemane. Under the laden branches of some gnarled tree, which was old when Isaiah was young, our Lord often spent the soft summer nights under the stars.

Any place may become an oratory or a private chapel, provided that one is able to find seclusion there. Isaac went into the fields to meditate (Genesis 24:63); Jacob lingered on the eastern bank of the river Jabbok after all his company had passed over (Genesis 32:22–24). It was there that he wrestled with the Angel and prevailed. Moses, hidden in the clefts of

Mount Horeb, beheld the vanishing glory that marked the way by which Jehovah had gone (Exodus 3:1–2). Elijah sent Ahab down to eat and drink while he himself withdrew to the lonely crest of Mount Carmel (1 Kings 18:42). Daniel spent weeks in an ecstasy of intercession on the banks of the Tigris River (Daniel 10:2–4). Paul, no doubt in order that he might have an opportunity for undisturbed meditation and prayer, made arrangements to travel on foot from Troas to Assos—a twenty-four-mile hike (Acts 20:13).

If no better place presents itself, the soul that turns to God may clothe itself in quietness even in the crowded concourse or in the hurrying streets. A poor woman in a great city, never able to free herself from the insistent clamor of her little ones, made for herself a sanctuary in the simplest way. "I throw my apron over my head," she said, "and there is my closet." On his return from the West Indies, Hewitson said, "I am not in want of a closet to pray in. I can just cover my face with my hat. There I am as much alone with God as in a closet."

The Quiet Hour

For most of us it may be harder to find the time than to find a place. I do not mean an "hour" of exactly sixty minutes, but a portion of time withdrawn from the engagements of the day, fenced round from the encroachments of business or pleasure, and dedicated to God. The "world's gray fathers" might linger in the fields in meditation on the covenant name until the evening hours. But we live with the clang of machinery and the roar of traffic always in our ears, and our crowding obligations jostle against each other as the hours fly by. We are often tempted to withdraw to other uses of those moments that we ought to hold sacred for communion with heaven.

Dr. Dale says somewhere that if each day had forty-eight hours, and every week had fourteen days, we might conceivably get through our work, but that, as things are, is impossible. There is at least an edge of truth in this whimsical utterance. Certainly, if we are to have a quiet hour set down in the midst of a hurry of duties, and to keep that time inviolate, we must exercise both planning and self-denial. We must be prepared to forego many things that are pleasant, and some things that are profitable. Let no one who can find time for their vanities say that they do not have enough time for prayer. We have to reclaim our time. It may be from recreation, or from social events, or from study, or from works of benevolence. Wherever it comes from, we must find time every day to enter into our closet, and having shut the door, to pray to our Father who is in secret.

John Wesley, in all his traveling, used to carry with him a little notebook for jottings, the first rude draft of his *Journals*. On the front page of each successive copy of this memorandum book he always recorded a resolution to spend two hours daily in private prayer, "no evasion or proviso being admitted." Perhaps such a rule may seem to some to be rigid, even a mere formality. Let no one be bound by another's practice, but in every case let due provision be made for communion with God.

One is tempted to linger here, and with all humility and earnestness to press the deliberation of this point. Some have been heard to say, "I confess that I do not spend much time in the secret chamber, but I try to cultivate the habit of continual prayer." The implication is that one is better than the other. The two ought not to be set in opposition. Each is necessary to a well-ordered Christian life. Each was perfectly maintained in the practice of the Lord Jesus. He was always encircled by the divine love; His communion with the Father was unbroken; He was the Son of Man who is in heaven.

Luke 5:16 tells us that is was His habit to withdraw himself into the wilderness and pray. The King James Version does not give us the force of the original Greek in this verse. Dean Vaughan comments on it: "It was not one withdrawal, nor one wilderness, nor one prayer—all is plural in the original—the withdrawals were repeated; the wildernesses were more than one, the prayers were habitual."

Crowds were swarming and pressing Him; great multitudes came together to hear and to be healed; and He had no time to so much as eat. Yet He found time to pray. This one who sought a retreat with so much thoughtful attention was the Son of God, having no sin to confess, no shortcoming to deplore, no unbelief to subdue, no lack of vigor to overcome. Nor are we to imagine that His prayers were merely peaceful meditations, or rapturous acts of communion. They were strenuous and warlike, from that hour in the wilderness when angels came to minister to the prostrate Man of Sorrows to that awful agony in which His sweat was like great drops of blood. His prayers were sacrifices, offered up with strong crying and tears.

Now, if it was part of the sacred discipline of the incarnate Son that He should observe frequent retreats, how much more is it incumbent upon us, broken as we are and disabled by a multitude of sins, to be diligent in the exercise of private prayer! To hurry over this duty would be to rob ourselves of the benefits that proceed from it. We know, of course, that prayer cannot be measured by divisions of time. But the advantages derived from secret prayer cannot be obtained unless we enter into it with deliberation. We must "shut the door," enclosing and securing a sufficient portion of time for the fitting discharge of the engagement before us.

In the morning we should look forward to the duties of the day, anticipating those situations in which temptation may lurk, and preparing ourselves to embrace such opportunities of usefulness as may be presented to us. In the evening we ought to remark upon the blessings that have come to us, consider our progress in holiness, and endeavor to profit by the lessons that God would have us learn. In addition, we must always acknowledge and forsake sin. Then there are the innumerable themes of prayer: the conversion and sanctification of our friends and acquaintances, the advancement of missionary effort, the health and growth of the Church of God, and the coming of the kingdom of Christ. All this cannot be pressed into a few crowded moments. We must be at leisure when we enter the secret place.

At one time at least in his life, the late Hudson Taylor was so fully occupied during the hours of the day with the direction of the China Inland Mission that he found it difficult to gain the requisite freedom for private prayer. Accordingly, he made it his rule to rise each night at two o'clock, watch with God till four, then lie down to sleep until the morning.

In the Jewish faith it was customary to set apart a space of time for meditation and prayer three times a day—in the morning, at noon, and in the evening (Psalm 55:17 and Daniel 6:10). In Bible lands there is a natural pause at midday which we, in our cooler climate, do not generally observe. Where it is possible to hallow a few moments in the midstream of the day's duties it ought surely to be done.

The Reverend James Fraser wrote in his memoirs: "Here I was counseled to set up one other sail, for before, I prayed but twice a day. I here resolved to set some time apart at midday for this effort, and, obeying this, I found the effects to be wonderful." Nature itself teaches us that morning and evening are suitable occasions of approach to God. A question that has been frequently asked is whether we should employ the morning or the evening hour for our more deliberate and prolonged period of waiting upon God. It is probable that each person can answer this question most profitably for him or herself. But it should always be understood that we give our best to God.

The Quiet Heart

For most of us, perhaps, it is most difficult to secure a stillness within the heart. The contemplationists of the Middle Ages desired to present themselves before God in silence that He might teach them what their lips should utter and their hearts expect. Stephen Gurnall acknowledges that it is far more difficult to hang up the big bell than it is to ring it after it has been hung. M'Cheyne used to say that much of his prayer time was spent in preparing to pray. Fraser gives a caution regarding this that is worth remembering. "Under the pretense of waiting on the Lord for strength, I have been driven to gaze, and neglect the duty itself, when there has been an opportunity; so in preparing for prayer have neglected prayer" (*Memoirs*, p. 290).

An English Puritan writes, "While I was at the Word, I saw I had a wild heart, which was as hard to stand and abide before the presence of God . . . as a bird before any man." Bunyan remarks from his own deep experiences, "Oh, the starting-holes that the heart has in the time of prayer, no one knows how many byways and back-lanes the heart finds to slip away from the presence of God." It was a saying of the martyr Bradford that "he would never leave a duty until he had brought his heart into the frame of that duty. He would not leave confession of sin until his heart was broken for sin. He would not leave petitioning for grace until his heart was quickened and enlivened in a hopeful expectation of more grace. He would not leave the giving of thanks until his heart was enlarged with a sense of the mercies that he enjoyed" (Bickerseth, *A Treatise on Prayer*, p. 93).

Keeping the Mind on God

There are three great but simple acts of faith that will enable us to focus our attention while in prayer. In the first place, we should recognize our acceptance before God through the dying of the Lord Jesus. When a pilgrim, either of the Greek or of the Latin Church, arrives in Jerusalem, his first act, before ever seeking refreshment or rest, is to visit the traditional scene of the Redeemer's passion. Our first act in prayer ought to be the yielding of our souls to the power of the blood of Christ. It was in the power of the ritual sacrifice that the high priest in Israel passed through the veil on the Day of Atonement. It is in the power of the accepted offering of the Lamb of divine appointment that we are privileged to come into the presence of God.

"Therefore, brothers, since we have confidence to enter the Most Holy Place by the blood of Jesus, by a new and living way opened for us through the curtain, that is, his body, and since we have a great priest over the house of God, let us draw near to God with a sincere heart in full assurance of faith, having our hearts sprinkled to cleanse us from a guilty conscience and having our bodies washed with pure water. Let us hold unswervingly to the hope we profess, for he who promised is faithful" (Hebrews 10:19–23).

Were I with the trespass laden
　　Of a thousand worlds beside,
Yet by that path I enter—
　　The blood of the Lamb who died.

It is important also that we confess and receive the enabling grace of the divine Spirit, without whom nothing is holy, nothing good. For it is He who teaches us to cry, "Abba, Father," who searches for us the deep things of God, who discloses to us the mind and will of Christ, who helps our infirmities, and intercedes on our behalf "according to God." Ambrose wrote, "This helping of the Spirit (Romans 8:26) is very emphatic in the original Greek. Like a man taking up a heavy piece of timber by one end, he cannot get it up by himself until some other man takes it up at the other end, so is the poor soul that is pulling and tugging with his own heart. Like the log in the ditch, he can do nothing with it until at last the Spirit of God comes at the other end, takes the heaviest of the burden, and so helps the soul to lift it up" (*Prima Media et Ultima*, p. 333).

Pére la Combe once said that he never found anyone who prayed so well as those who had never been taught how. Those who have no master in man have one in the Holy Spirit. "And we, who with unveiled faces all reflect the Lord's glory, are being transformed into his likeness with ever-increasing glory, which comes from the Lord, who is the Spirit" (2 Corinthians 3:18). When we enter the inner chamber we should present ourselves before God with meekness and promise, and open our hearts to the incoming and infilling of the Holy Spirit. We shall receive from the praying Spirit, and commit to the praying Christ, those petitions that are of divine birth. They express themselves through our finite hearts and sin-stained lips in "groanings which cannot be uttered."

Without the support of the Holy Spirit, prayer becomes a matter of incredible difficulty. "As for my heart," said one who was deeply involved in this engagement, "when I go to pray, I find it reluctant to go to God. When it is with Him, reluctant to stay with Him. Many times I am forced in my prayers, first to beg of God that He would take my heart and set it on himself in Christ, and when it is there that He would keep it there. I know not what to pray for, I am so blind, nor how to pray, I am so ignorant; only, blessed be grace, the Spirit helps our infirmities."

It is well for us to begin our supplications by directing our hearts toward the Holy Scriptures because these are His chosen means of enlightenment, comfort, inspiration, and rebuke. It will greatly help to calm the stubborn and contrary mind if we open the sacred volume and read as if in the presence of God. We should remain there until a word from the Eternal comes to us from the printed page. George Müller confessed that he often could not pray until he had steadied his mind upon a text. Is it not the prerogative of God to break the silence? "Thou hast said, 'Seek ye my face.' My heart says to thee, 'Thy face, LORD, do I seek' " (Psalm 27:8, RSV). Is it not fitting that His will should order all the acts of our communication with Him? Let us be silent before God that He may fashion us.

So shall I keep
For ever in my heart one silent space;
A little sacred spot of loneliness,
Where to set up the memory of Thy Cross,
A little quiet garden, where no man
May pass or rest forever, sacred still
To visions of Thy sorrow and Thy love.

Thou ought to go to prayer, that thou may deliver thyself wholly up into the hands of God, with perfect resignation, exerting an act of faith, believing that thou art in the divine Presence, afterward settling in that holy repose, with quietness, silence, and tranquility; and endeavoring for a whole day, a whole year, and thy whole life, to continue that first act of contemplation by faith and love.

—Molinos

Satan strikes either at the root of faith or at the root of diligence.

—John Livingstone

The sum is: Remember always the presence of God; rejoice always in the will of God; and direct all to the glory of God.

—Archbishop Leighton

3
The Direction of the Mind

In Essex, in the year 1550, a number of religious persons who had received the Word of God as their only rule of faith and conduct, and who therefore differed in certain particulars from the dominant party in the church, met to confer on the order of worship. The chief point in debate related to the attitude that one ought to observe in prayer—whether it was better to stand or kneel, and whether to have the head covered or uncovered. They decided that the material question had reference not to the bodily posture, but to the direction of the mind. It was agreed that the best attitude was the one that most fitly expresses the desires and emotions of the soul.

Realize the Presence of God

He who fills earth and heaven *is,* in a singular and impressive sense, in the secret place. As the electric fluid that is diffused in the atmosphere is concentrated in the lightning flash, so the presence of God becomes vivid and powerful in the prayer chamber. "Always enter upon prayer by putting yourself in the divine Presence" (Francois de Sales). Gaston de Renty defines this posture of the soul as "a state of modest presence before God, in which you maintain yourself looking to His Spirit to suggest what He pleases to you, and receiving it in simplicity and confidence, just as if He were uttering words in your hearing." Avila, a Spanish writer on religion, tells us that "we ought to address ourselves to prayer in order to listen rather than to speak." Bishop Jeremy Taylor enforces this rule with stately and affluent speech: "In the beginning of actions of religion, make an act of adoration; that is, solemnly worship God, and place yourself in God's presence. Behold Him with the eye of faith; and let your desires actually fix on Him as the object of your worship, the reason of your hope, and the fountain of your blessing. For when you have placed yourself before Him and are kneeling in His presence, it is most likely that all the following parts of your devotion will be answerable to the wisdom of such an understanding, and the glory of such a presence."

Our Father *is* in the secret place. We shall find Him in the inwardness of a "recollected" spirit, in the stillness of a heart united to fear His name. The dew falls most copiously when the night winds are hushed. The great tides lift themselves "too full for sound or foam." The supplicant who prays with a true direction of spirit, "Our Father, who art in heaven," is oftentimes taken up into heaven before he is even aware. "But, oh, how rare it is!" cries Fénelon. "How rare it is to find a soul quiet enough to hear God speak!"

So many of us have untrained ears. We are like the Indian hunters of whom Whittier speaks, who can hear the crackle of a twig far off in the dim forest, but are deaf to the thunder of Niagara only a few yards away. Brother Lawrence, who lived to practice the presence of God, wrote, "As for my set hours of prayer, they are only a continuation of the same exercise. Sometimes I consider myself like a stone before a carver who is going to make a statue. Presenting myself before God I desire Him to form His perfect image in my soul, and make me entirely like himself. At other times, when I apply myself to prayer, I feel all my spirit and all my soul lift itself up without any care or effort of my own. It continues as if it were suspended and firmly fixed in God as its center and place of rest." The realization of the divine Presence is the inflexible condition of a right engagement of spirit in the exercise of private prayer.

John Spilsbury of Bromgrove, who was confined in Worcester jail for the testimony of Christ, bore this witness: "I shall not, from this time on, fear prison as before, because I had so much of my Heavenly Father's company it was made as a palace to me." Another, in a similar case, testified: "I thought of Jesus until every stone in my cell shone like a ruby." For us, too, in our measure, the dull room in which we talk with God, as a man may speak with his friend, will burn at times like a sapphire. It will be to us like the rifted rock in Sinai, through which the uncreated glory poured, until the prophet's steadfast gaze was dimmed, and his countenance kindled as a flame.

Our realization of the presence of God may, however, be accompanied with little or no emotion. Our spirits may lie as if dead under the hand of God. Vision and rapture may alike be withdrawn. But this ought not cause us to grow languid in prayer. Instead of becoming discouraged and intermittent with our exercise at such times, we ought to redouble our energy. It may be that the prayer which goes up through darkness to God will bring to us a blessing such as we have not received in our most favored hours. The prayer that rises from "the land of forgetfulness," "the place of darkness," "the belly of hell," may have an abundant and glorious return.

At the same time, there are seasons of special privilege when the winds of God are unbound about the throne of grace, and the breath of spring begins to stir in the King's gardens. The Scots Worthies used to talk much of gaining *access*. It is told that when two visitors presented themselves before Robert Bruce on a certain morning, he said to them, "You must go and leave me for some time. I thought last night when I lay down that I had a good measure of the Lord's presence, and now I have wrestled the last hour or two and have not yet got access." It may be that in his solicitude there was a disproportionate subjectivity, yet the eagerness of his desire was surely commendable. To what profit is it that we dwell in Jerusalem if we do not see the King's face? When He comes out from His royal chambers, accompanied with blessing, should we not make ourselves available that we may yield Him worship and offer Him service? Jonathan Edwards resolved that whenever he should find himself "in a good frame for divine contemplation," he would not allow even the recurrence of the midday meal to interrupt his engagement with His Lord. "I will forego my dinner," he said, "rather than be broken off." When the fire of God glowed upon Mt. Carmel, it was Ahab who went down to eat and drink . . . it was Elijah who went up to pray.

Honesty Is Imperative

He who *is* in the secret place sees in secret when we kneel in His pure presence. In our address to God we like to speak of Him as we think we ought to speak, and there are times when our words far outrun our feelings. But it is best that we should be perfectly frank before Him. He will allow us to say anything we will, so long as we say it to Him. "I say to God my Rock," exclaims the psalmist, 'Why have you forgotten me?' " (Psalm 42:9). If he had said, "Lord, you cannot forget me: you have chiseled my name on the palms of your hands," he would have spoken more worthily, but less truly. On one occasion Jeremiah failed to interpret God correctly. He cried, as if in anger, "O Lord, you deceived me, and I was deceived; you overpowered me and prevailed" (Jeremiah 20:7). These are terrible words to utter before Him who is changeless truth. But the prophet spoke as he felt, and the Lord not only pardoned him, He met and blessed him there.

It is possible that some who read these words may have a complaint against God. A controversy of long standing has come between your soul and His grace. If you were to say the word that is trembling on your lips, you would say to Him, "Why have you dealt with me this way?" Then dare to say, with reverence and with boldness, all that is in your heart. " 'Present your case,' says the Lord. 'Set forth your arguments,' says Jacob's King" (Isaiah 41:21). Carry your grievance into the light of His countenance, drive your complaint home. Then listen to His answer. For surely, in gentleness and truth, He will clear himself of the charge of unkindness that you bring against Him. In His light you shall see light. However, remember that this is a private matter between you and your Lord. You must not defame Him to anyone. "If I had said, 'I will speak thus,' I would have betrayed your children" (Psalm 73:15). John Livingstone of Ancrum, in a day of darkness, made a most excellent resolution, "Finding myself, as I thought, surely deserted and somewhat harshly dealt with in my particular state, I made a promise to God not to tell it to any but himself, lest I should seem to complain or foster misbelief in myself or others."

There is another region in which honesty in prayer must operate. There have been times, no doubt, in the life of each one of us, when the Spirit of God granted us enlargement of affection and desire. Our prayers soared through heavenly distances, and were about to fold their wings before the throne. When, suddenly, there was brought to our remembrance some duty unfulfilled, some harmful indulgence tolerated, some sin unrepented of. It was in order that we might forsake that which is evil, and follow that which is good, that the Holy Spirit granted us so abundantly His assistance in prayer. "Prayer discovers for us the true state of our soul, for according to theologians, it is the mirror that shows us our correct portrait" (St. John Climacus, *The Holy Ladder of Perfection*, 28:38).

God designed it so that in the good hour of His visitation, we should be enabled to purify ourselves from every stain, in order that henceforth we might live as His "purchased possession." Perhaps, in such a case, we shunned the light and turned back from the solicitation of God. Then darkness fell upon our face, and the divine Comforter who "helps us in our weakness" (Romans 8:26), being grieved, withdrew. To that hour, it may be, we can trace our present feebleness in the holy exercise of prayer. "If I had cherished sin in my heart, the Lord would not have listened" (Psalm 66:18). "If anyone turns a deaf ear to the law, even his prayers are detestable" (Proverbs 28:9). "But your iniquities have separated you from your God; your sins have hidden his face from you, so that he will not hear" (Isaiah 59:2). "When you spread out your hands in prayer, I will hide my eyes from you; even if you offer many prayers, I will not listen" (Isaiah 1:15).

In wireless telegraphy if the receiver is not attuned to the transmitter, communication is impossible. In true prayer God and the suppliant must be of one accord. Cavalier, a Huguenot leader, who had lived for years in the enjoyment of unbroken communion with God, was deceived by vanity and forsook the cause to which he had devoted his life. Finally, he came to England and entered the British army. When he was presented to Queen Anne, she said, "Does God visit you now, Monsieur Cavalier?" The young Camisard bowed his head and was silent.

Christmas Evans tells of an eclipse of faith that he experienced. A time of powerlessness and decay followed, but the Lord visited him in mercy. "Lazarus had been dead four days when Jesus came that way." Immediately he began to plead that the fervor and gladness of earlier years might be restored. "On the Caerphilly mountain," he relates, "the spirit of prayer fell upon me, as it had once in Anglesea. I wept and supplicated, and gave myself to Christ. I wept long and besought Jesus Christ, and my heart poured forth its requests before Him on the mountain." Then followed a period of marvelous blessing.

On the other hand, "If our hearts do not condemn us, we have confidence before God and receive from him anything we ask, because we obey his commands and do what pleases him" (1 John 3:21–22).

The devotional writers of the Middle Ages were accustomed to distinguish between "a pure intention" and "a right intention." The former, they said, was the fruit of sanctification, the latter was the condition of sanctification. The former implied a trained and disciplined will, the latter a will laid down in meek surrender at the Master's feet. Now, what God requires of those who seek His face is "a right intention"—a deliberate, a resigned, a joyful acceptance of His good and perfect will. All true prayer must fall back upon the great atonement, in which the Man of Sorrows translated into "active passion" the supplication of His agony. "My Father, if it is possible, may this cup be taken from me. Yet not as I will, but as you will" (Matthew 26:39). He has transmitted to us His own prayer and we offer it in the power of His sacrifice. "This, then, is how you should pray: 'Our Father in heaven . . . your will be done' " (Matthew 6:9–10).

Lord, here I hold within my trembling hand,
 This will of mine—a thing which seemeth small;
And only Thou, O Christ, canst understand
 How, when I yield Thee this, I yield mine all.
It hath been wet with tears, and stained with sighs,
 Clenched in my grasp till beauty has it none;
Now, from Thy footstool where it prostrate lies
 The prayer ascendeth, Let Thy will be done.

The Necessity of Faith

"Do not be afraid, little flock, for your Father has been pleased to give you the kingdom" (Luke 12:32). "Your Father knows what you need" (Matthew 6:8). "The Father himself loves you" (John 16:27). The whole philosophy of prayer is contained in words like these. "This word 'Father,' " writes Luther, "has overcome God."

Let it be once admitted that because God is, no miracle is impossible. Let it be acknowledged that He is the rewarder of them that diligently seek Him; no true prayer will remain unblessed. However, faith in God is by no means an effortless or idle activity. Robert Bruce of Edinburgh used to pause in his preaching, and bending over the pulpit, say with much solemnity, "I think it's a great matter to believe there is a God." Once he confessed that during three years he never said "my God" without being "challenged and disquieted for the same." "These words, 'My God,' " said Ebenezer Erskine, "are the marrow of the Gospel." To be able to hold the living God within our feeble grasp, and say with assurance, "God, even our own God, shall bless us" (Psalm 67:6, KJV), demands a faith that is not of nature's birth.

It is comforting to remember that even a feeble faith prevails to overcome. "Is it not a wonder," says Robert Blair, "that our words in prayer, which almost die in the coming out of our lips, should climb so well as to go into heaven?"

It is indeed a wonder, but all the doings of God in grace are wondrous. Like the miner, whose trained eye detects the glitter of the precious metal sown in sparse flakes through the coarse grain of the rocks, God observes the rare but costly faith that lies imbedded in our unbelief. Standing somewhere on the slopes of "that goodly mountain" Hermon, our Lord said to His disciples, "If you have faith as small as a mustard seed, you can say to this mountain, 'Move from here to there' and it will move. Nothing will be impossible for you" (Matthew 17:20). The mountain that the word of faith was to pluck up and cast into the sea was the immeasurable mass that fills the horizon to the north of Palestine, whose roots run under the whole land of Immanuel, and whose dew refreshes the city of God.

Faith, mighty faith, the promise sees,
And looks to that alone;
Laughs at impossibilities,
And cries, It shall be done.

When the pilgrims came to the Delectable Mountains, the shepherds showed them a man standing on Mount Marvel who "tumbled the hills about with words." That man was the son of one Mr. Great Grace, the King's champion, and he was set there "to teach pilgrims to believe down, or to tumble out of their way what difficulties they should meet with, by faith."

This God who is ours is our Father. Our Lord confers on us His own rights and privileges. He puts into our hand the master key, which unlocks all the doors of the treasury of God. "No matter how many promises God has made, they are 'Yes' in Christ. And so through him the 'Amen' is spoken by us to the glory of God" (2 Corinthians 1:20). In Him we draw nigh to God. To Him we refer with boldness our requests. Ralph Erskine tells us that, on a certain Sabbath evening, he had unusual liberty in prayer through the name of the Lord Jesus. "I was helped to pray in secret with an outpouring of the soul before the Lord, owning my claim to the promise, my claim to pardon, my claim to grace, my claim to daily bread, my claim to a comfortable life, my claim to a songless death, my claim to a glorious resurrection, and my claim to everlasting life and happiness: to be *only* in Christ, and in God through Him as a promising God."

When we pray to our Father we offer our prayers in the name of Jesus—with His authority. We must not think, however, that the name of Jesus may be used by us however we are inclined. God can in no wise deal with His children as King Xerxes dealt with Mordecai when he handed him the great seal with the words, "Write . . . as seems best to you, and seal it with the king's signet ring—for no document written in the king's name and sealed with his ring can be revoked" (Esther 8:8).

John Bunyan shows his accustomed spiritual discernment when in his *Holy War*, he writes about the petitions that the men of Mansoul sent to Emmanuel, to none of which He returned any answer. After a time "they agreed together to draw up yet another petition, and to send it away to Emmanuel for relief. But Mr. Godly-Fear stood up and answered that he knew his Lord, the Prince, never did, nor ever would, receive a petition for these matters from the hand of any whoever unless the Lord Secretary's hand was to it. 'And this,' he quotes, 'is the reason you prevailed not all this while.' Then they said they would draw one up, and get the Lord Secretary's hand to it. But Mr. Godly-Fear answered again that he knew also that the Lord Secretary would not set His hand to any petition that himself had not a hand in composing and drawing up." Bishop Wescott later wrote, "The petitions of believers . . . are echoes, so to speak, of the Master's own words. Their prayer is only some fragment of His teaching transformed into a supplication. It must then be heard, for it is the expression of His will."

The prayer of faith is a middle term between the intercession of the Holy Spirit and the intercession of Christ. "Prayer is heard when it passes from the believer's heart to the Redeemer's heart, and is appropriated by the Redeemer, or made His own" (Hewitson, *Life*, p. 375). It is the divinely appointed means by which the unutterable groanings of the Spirit, who dwells within His people as in a temple, are conveyed and committed to the exalted Mediator, who "ever liveth to make intercession" for us. Thus in a peculiar and exceptional way, by the grace of God, those who make mention of the Lord become fellow-laborers together with God.

We praise Thee. . . . We give thanks to Thee for Thy great glory, O Lord God.

—*Book of Common Prayer*

Were there nothing else
For which to praise the heavens but only love,
That only love were cause enough for praise.

—*Tennyson*

Praise Him, ever praise Him,
For remembering dust of earth.

—*Morgan Rhys*

4
The Engagement: Worship

When you have shut your door, PRAY. The word used here, that word which is most frequently employed in the New Testament to denote prayer, implies a desire *toward*. While it suggests petition, it is sufficiently general to include the whole of our engagement in the secret place—worship, confession, request. In this chapter we shall speak of the first of these—worship.

When Scipio Africanus entered Rome, after he had humbled the proud city of Carthage, he rode in procession along the Way of Triumph, swept over the Velia, passed reverently down the ancient Way of Sacrifice, and then climbed the long ascent of the Capitol, scattering with both hands "the gold coins of the victor," while the air was torn with the tumultuous ovations of the crowd. Amid the rejoicing multitudes there were probably some whose most obvious sentiment of gratitude was stirred by the generosity of the conqueror in that hour of triumph. Others exulted in the rolling away of the terror of years, and thought with emotion of the fair fields of Italy now freed from the yoke of the stranger. Others, forgetting for the moment personal benefits or national enlargement, acclaimed the specific qualities of the victor—his resourcefulness, his magnanimity, his courage, his courtesy.

Similarly, the tribute of praise that the saints are instructed to render to the Lord may arise either in the acknowledgment of daily mercies, in thanksgiving for the great redemption, or in contemplation of the divine perfection.

Remembrance

"Memory," says Aristotle, "is the scribe of the soul." Let her bring forth her tablets, and write. Fraser of Brea, at one time a prisoner for Christ's sake on the Bass Rock, resolved that he would search out and record the lovingkindnesses of God. He did so with a very happy effect upon his own spirit. He says, "The calling to mind and seriously meditating on the Lord's dealings with me as to soul and body and on His manifold mercies has done me very much good. It has cleared my case, confirmed my soul of God's love and my interest in Him, and made me love Him. Oh . . . what wells of water have my eyes been opened to see, which before were hidden. Scarcely anything has done me more good than this."

Let us take the trouble to observe and consider the Lord's dealings with us, and we shall surely receive soul-enriching views of His kindness and truth. His mercies are new every morning. His works make the evening a time for rejoicing. His thoughts concerning us are as numerous as the sands on the shore, and they are all thoughts of peace. Those benefits that recur with so much regularity that they seem to us common and ordinary, which interweave with golden threads the homespun garment of our daily life, ought to be most lovingly commemorated. Often these blessings are unspeakably great.

"I have experienced today the most exquisite pleasure that

I have ever had in my life," said a young invalid. "I was able to breathe freely for about five minutes." In Dr. Judson's house in Burma some friends were speculating on the highest form of happiness that could come from outside circumstances, and each fortified their own opinion by the citing of some authority. "Pooh," said Dr. Judson, who had been recalling his terrible imprisonment in Ava, "these men are not qualified to judge. What do you think of floating down the Irrawadi, on a cool, moonlit evening, with your wife by your side and your baby in your arms? Free, all free? But you cannot understand it either. It needs twenty-one months worth of qualification. I can scarcely regret my twenty-one months of misery when I recall that one delicious thrill. I think I have had a better appreciation of what heaven may be like ever since." How often do we thank God for the mere joy of living in the free and healthful use of all our faculties?

"The river past, and God forgotten," is an English proverb that should never apply to those who have tasted that the Lord is gracious. "It is fitting for the upright to praise him" (Psalm 33:1) is the judgment of the Old Testament; "In everything give thanks" (1 Thessalonians 5:18, KJV) is the decision of the New. Richard Baxter advises that on Sabbath days we should be briefer in confession and lamentation, and give ourselves more to praise and thanksgiving (*Method of Peace and Comfort*). It was Grimshaw's custom to begin his morning devotions by singing the doxology. Of Joseph Alleine it was said, "Such was the vehement heavenliness of his spirit that his favorite employment was praise." Even a heathen was moved to say, "What can I, a lame old man, do but sing His praise, and exhort others to do the same?" (Epictetus, *Encheiridion*, p. 16). For the beauty of nature, the fellowship of the good, the tender love of home; for safe conduct in temptation, strength to overcome, deliverance from evil; for the generosity, the patience, the sympathy of God;

and for ten thousand unobserved or unremembered mercies, let us unflaggingly bless His Holy Name. "Give thanks to the Lord, for he is good. His love endures forever" (Psalm 136:1).

However, if things go hard with us, and trials darken all our sky, are we still to give thanks and bless our God? Of course!

> Trials make the promise sweet;
> Trials give new life to prayer;
> Trials bring me to His feet,
> Lay me low, and keep me there.

Let us thank God for our poverty. We dwell, perhaps, in a land of narrowness. But like Immanuel Kant's garden, it is "endlessly high." The air is fresh, and the sun is clear. The winter is frosty, but kind. With the springtime comes the singing of birds, and the bloom and fragrance of flowers. If even in the summer there breathes "a nipping and an eager air," there is always the health-giving smile of God. On the other hand, how true is the thought of Augustine, "Earthly riches are full of poverty." Rich stores of corn and wine will never satiate a hungry soul. Purple and fine linen may only mask a threadbare life. The shrill blare of fame's trumpet cannot subdue the discords of the spirit. The best night that Jacob ever spent was when a stone was his pillow and the skies the curtains of his tent. When Jacob was held in derision by youths whose fathers he would have disdained to put with the dogs of his flock, he was made a spectacle to angels, and became the theme of their wonder and joy. The defeat that Adam sustained in Paradise, the Redeemer retrieved in the desolation of the desert and the anguish of His passion. The cross we are called to bear may be heavy, but we do not have to carry it far. When God bids us to lay it down, heaven begins.

Chrysostom on his way to exile exclaimed, "Thank God for everything!" If we imitate him we shall never have a bad day. Alexander Simson, a famous Scottish minister of two hundred years ago, when out walking once, fell and broke his leg. He was found "sitting with his broken leg in his arm, and crying out, 'Blessed be the Lord; blessed be His name.' " Truly, seeing that all things work together for good to those who love God, he was wise. Richard Baxter found reason to bless God for a discipline of pain that endured for thirty-five years. Samuel Rutherford exclaimed, "Oh, what I owe to the furnace, the trial, and the hammer of my Lord Jesus!"

Thanksgiving

All our mercies, rightly viewed, lead us back to the thought of our acceptance in Christ. The river of the water of life, which makes the desert glad, flows from under the throne of God and the Lamb. The benefits of that gracious covenant are all confirmed for our use and pleasure by the seal of His blood.

There's not a gift His hand bestows,
 But cost His heart a groan.

The water may be spent in the bottle, but the Well of the Oath is springing freshly just at hand. It is so near that we may hear the music of its flow. Thieves may rob us of our spending money, "but our gold is in our trunk at home." God may take away from us much that is dear, but has He not already given us Christ? In whatever way the prayer of thanksgiving may circle in and out among the gracious providences of God, it will infallibly come to rest at the feet of the Lord.

To praise Christ is a high exercise. What Thomas Boston

says of preaching is also true of praising: "I saw the preaching of Christ to be the most difficult thing. Even though the whole world is full of wonders, yet here are depths beyond all." Seeing it to be so he kept this "suit" pending before God for a long time, "that he might see Christ by a spiritual illumination." So eager was he for the acceptance of his plea, and so grievous to his soul was his ignorance of Christ, that his bodily health began to be affected. Yet, as he tells us, there were times when his soul went out in love to Christ, followed hard after Him, and "saw much content, delight, and sweetness in Him."

The Passover in Israel was celebrated on the eve of the great deliverance, which was from that time forward a "night to be much observed unto the Lord." Let us frequently commemorate our redemption from a bondage more bitter than that of Egypt. John Bunyan conveys this wholesome counsel to his "dear children": "Call to mind the former days and years of ancient times, remember also your songs in the night, and commune with your own hearts. Look diligently, and leave no corner unsearched for that hidden treasure, even the treasure of your first and second experience of the grace of God toward you. Remember I say, the word that first laid hold upon you. Remember your terror of conscience and fear of death and hell. Remember also your tears and prayers to God—oh, how you sighed under every hedge for mercy! Don't you have a hill *Mizar* to remember? Have you forgotten the closet, the milkhouse, the stable, the barn and the like, where God visited your souls? Remember also the Word. The word, I say, upon which the Lord caused you to hope."

It is right that we should search into the riches and glory of the inheritance of which we have been make partakers. The blood of Christ, the grace of the Spirit, the light of the divine countenance, are "three jewels worth more than heaven." Chrysostom proclaimed that "the name of Christ has in it ten thousand treasures of joy." When we recall the mercies that are made sure to us "in the blood of an eternal covenant," perhaps the most acceptable form of worship and the swiftest incitement to praise is the act of appropriation by which we consider ourselves heirs to the purchased possession already ours in Christ. Dr. Chalmers was one of those who had discovered this open secret. In his diary we frequently meet with expressions such as these: "Began my first waking minutes with a confident hold of Christ as my Savior. A day of great quietness." "Let the laying hold of Christ as my propitiation be the unvarying initial act of every morning." "Began the day with a distinct act of confidence, but should renew it through the day." "Began again with an act of confidence, but why not a perennial confidence in the Savior?" "I have returned more frequently to the acts of faith in Christ, and I have no doubt that this habit will bring me to the right." "Returning to the topic of a great confidence and belief in the promises of the Gospel, let me act on the injunction, 'Open your mouth wide, and I will fill it.' "

It is our pleasant duty also to review with thanksgiving all the ways by which the Lord has led us. Otto Funcke has beautifully entitled his brief autobiography, *The Footprints of God in the Pathway of My Life*. The way of the divine direction may lead from the bitter waters of Marah to the tempered shade of Elims' palms. It may pass through the fiery desert, but it reaches onward to the Mount of God. It may descend to the valley of the shadow of death, but it will bring us out and through to the pleasant land of the promises of God.

A land of corn and wine and oil,
Favored with God's peculiar smile,
With every blessing blest.

In that "right way" of the divine conduct there is always the comforting and awesome presence of our great God and Savior. We cannot recall the mercies we received along the way and not remember Him. He took, with a hand that was pierced, the bitter cup, and drank until His lips were wet with our sorrow and doom. Now the cup of bitterness has become sweet. Where His footsteps fell the wilderness rejoiced, and the waste places of our life became as fruitful as Carmel. A rugged track beneath our feet ran darkly into the night, but the tender love of His presence was as a lamp to our feet and light upon our path. His name is fragrance; His voice is music; His countenance is health. Dr. Judson, in his last illness, had a wonderful entrance into the land of praise. He would suddenly exclaim, as the tears ran down his face, "Oh, the love of Christ! the love of Christ! We cannot understand it now, but what a beautiful study for eternity." Again and again, though his pain was constant and severe, he would cry in a holy rapture, "Oh, the love of Christ! the love of Christ!"

Such praises uplift their strain until it mingles with the glory of the new song that fills the sanctuary on high, "You are worthy to take the scroll and to open its seals, because you were slain, and with your blood you purchased men for God from every tribe and language and people and nation. You have made them to be a kingdom and priests to serve our God, and they will reign on the earth" (Revelation 5:9–10).

Contemplation

Praise addressed to God in name and memory of Jesus Christ rises inevitably into adoration. It is here that most often "praise is silent." Isaiah, transported by faith into the inner sanctuary, was rapt into the worship of the seraphim, and joined in spirit in the unending adoration of the triune God. "Holy, holy, holy is the Lord Almighty; the whole earth is full of his glory" (Isaiah 6:3). The herald angels poured forth upon the plains of Bethlehem the song of heaven, "Glory to God in the highest!" Our sad earth heard it and was comforted.

> Angels, help us to adore Him;
> Ye behold Him face to face!

But even these bright intelligences were unable to show forth all His praise. John Livingstone wrote in his diary on December 14, 1634: "No doubt the angels think themselves insufficient for the praises of the Lord."

It is reported of John Janeway that many times in the hour of secret prayer he scarcely knew whether he was "in the body, or out of the body." Tersteegen said to some friends who had gathered round him, "I sit here and talk with you, but within is the eternal adoration, unceasing and undisturbed." Wodrow relates that on one occasion Mr. Carstairs was invited to take part in communion services at Calder, near Glasgow. He was wonderfully assisted and had "a strange gale through all the sermon." His hearers were affected in an unusual degree, as glory seemed to fill the house. "A Christian man that had been at the table and was obliged to come out of the church pressed to get in again but could not succeed for some time. So he stood outside the door, wrapped up in the thoughts of the glory that was in the house for nearly half an hour, and could think of nothing else."

Dr. A. J. Gordon describes the impression made upon his mind by talking with Joseph Rabinowitz, whom Dr. Delitzsch considered the most remarkable Jewish convert since Saul of Tarsus. "We shall not soon forget the radiance that would come onto his face as he expounded the Messianic psalms at our morning or evening worship. Here and there, as he caught a glimpse of the suffering or glorified Christ, he would suddenly lift his hands and his eyes to heaven in a burst of admiration, exclaiming with Thomas after he had seen the nailprints, 'My Lord, and my God!' "

For many of us, emotion may be feeble and rapture of the spirit may be rare. Love to Christ may express itself more naturally in right conduct than in a tumult of praise. But it is probable that to each sincere believer there are granted seasons of communion when, as one turns to the unseen glory, the veil of sense becomes translucent. One seems to behold within the holiest the very face and form of Him who died for our sins, who rose for our justification, who now awaits us at the right hand of God. Even so, we must never forget that adoration does not exhaust itself in pleasing emotions. By the law of its nature it turns again to request: "Our Father which art in heaven, *Hallowed be thy name*" (Matthew 6:9, KJV).

The garden of spices is sprinkled with red flowers.

—Heinrich Seuse

It is a great and rare thing to have forgiveness in God discovered unto a sinful soul. . . . It is a pure Gospel truth that hath neither shadow, footstep, nor imitation elsewhere. The whole creation hath not the least obscure impression of it left thereon.

—John Owen

5
The Engagement: Confession

Before His breath the bands
That held me fall and shrivel up in flame.
He bears my name upon His wounded hands,
  Upon His heart my name.
  I wait, my soul doth wait
For Him who on His shoulder bears the Key;
I sit fast bound, and yet not desolate;
  My mighty Lord is free.
  Be thou uplifted, Door
Of everlasting strength! The Lord on high
Hath gone, and captive led forevermore
  My long captivity.

—Dora Greenwell

"If we confess our sins, he is faithful and just and will forgive us our sins and purify us from all unrighteousness" (1 John 1:9). Confession of sin is the first act of an awakened sinner, the first mark of a gracious spirit. When God desires a habitation in which to dwell, He prepares "a broken and a contrite heart." The altar of reconciliation stands at the entrance of the New Testament temple. From the altar the worshiper passes on, by way of the laver, to the appointed place of meeting—the blood-stained mercy seat.

Now we speak of the confession of sin, which is due by those who are justified, having found acceptance in Christ Jesus. Though they are children, they are still sinners. If they walk in the light, they are conscious—as in their unregenerate state they never were—of the turpitude of their guilt, and the hatefulness of their iniquity. For now they bring their transgression and apostasies into the light of God's countenance. Holding them up before Him, they cry, "Against you, you only, have I sinned and done what is evil in your sight, so that you are proved right when you speak and justified when you judge" (Psalm 51:4).

Confession of sin should be explicit. "The care of Christianity is for particulars," says Bishop Warburton. The ritual law in Israel that provided for the transference of sin on the Day of Atonement presupposed definition in confession. "He [the high priest] is to lay both hands on the head of the live goat and confess over it all the wickedness and rebellion of the Israelites—all their sins" (Leviticus 16:21). In private sacrifices also, while the hands of the offerer were laid on the victim (Leviticus 1:4), the following prayer was recited: "I entreat, O Jehovah: I have sinned, I have done perversely, I have rebelled, I have committed ____________." Then the special sin or sins were named and the worshiper continued, "But I return in penitence. Let this be for my atonement." Standing beside the ruins of Jericho, Joshua said to Achan, "My son, give glory to the Lord, the God of Israel, and give him the praise. Tell me what you have done; do not hide it from me. Achan replied, 'It is true! I have sinned against the Lord, the God of Israel. This is what I have done:' " (Joshua 7:19–20). The great promise of the New Testament is not any less definite. "If we confess our sins, he is faithful and just and will forgive us our sins and purify us from all unrighteousness" (1 John 1:9). A wise old writer says, "A child of God will confess sin in particular. An unsound Christian will confess sin indiscriminately. He will acknowledge he is a sinner in general, but David pointed his finger to the sore and said, 'Against thee, only thee, have I done *this* evil in thy sight' (Psalm 51:4, KJV). He does not say, 'I have done evil,' but '*this* evil.' He points to his bloodguiltiness."

When, in the course of the day's engagements, our conscience witnesses against us that we have sinned, we should at once confess our guilt, claim by faith the cleansing of the blood of Christ, and so wash our hands in innocence. Afterward, as soon as we have a convenient opportunity, we ought to review with deliberation the wrong that we have done. As we consider it with God we should be impressed by its evil qualities, because we obviously were not so inclined at the time we committed it. If the sin is one that we have committed before, one to which perhaps our nature lies open, we must cast ourselves in utter faith upon the strong mercy of God, pleading with Him in the name of Christ that we may never again so grieve Him. John Owen exhorted us to "think of the guilt of sin that you may be humbled. Think of the power of sin that you may seek strength against it. Think not of the matter of sin . . . lest you be more and more entangled."

As our hearts grow more tender in the presence of God, the remembrance of former sins, which have already been acknowledged and forgiven, will from time to time imprint a fresh stain upon our conscience. In such a case, nature itself seems to teach us that we ought again to implore the pardoning grace of God. For we bend, not before the judgment seat of the divine Lawgiver, but before our Father, to whom we have been reconciled through Christ. A more adequate conception of the offense that we have committed ought surely to be followed by a deeper penitence for the wrong done. Under the guidance of the Holy Spirit we shall often be led to pray with the psalmist, "Remember not the sins of my youth" (Psalm 25:7), even though these have long since been dealt with and done away. Conviction of sin will naturally prompt us toward confession. When such promptings are disregarded, the spirit who has wrought in us that conviction is grieved.

My sins, my sins, my Savior,
    How sad on Thee they fall;
While through Thy gentle patience
    I tenfold feel them all.
I know they are forgiven;
    But still their pain to me
Is all the grief and anguish
    They laid, my Lord, on Thee.

It is of the first importance that in all the exercises of the secret chamber, we should yield ourselves to the blessed influences of the Comforter. He alone enables us to pray with acceptance. An important caution in regard to this has been noted by Ralph Erskine. In his diary he writes, under the date January 23, 1733, "This morning . . . I was quickened in prayer, and strengthened to hope in the Lord. At the beginning of my prayer I discerned a lively frame of mind, which asserted God in Christ to be the fountain of my life, the strength of my life, and the joy of my life. I discovered that I had no life that deserved that name unless He himself were my life. Checking myself with reflections upon my own sinfulness, vileness, and corruption, I began to acknowledge my wickedness; but then the sweet frame of mind failed me and wore off. From this I may gather this lesson, that no sweet influence of the Spirit ought to be held back on the pretense of getting a better frame of mind founded upon humiliation; otherwise, the Lord may be provoked to withdraw."

When Thomas Boston found himself in danger of giving way to excessive pride, he took a look at his black heart. It was said of Charles Simeon, of Cambridge, that in his private hours he was particularly broken and prostrate before the Lord. We may well do the same, but never so as to lose our assurance of sonship, or our sense of the preciousness of Christ. As Rutherford reminds us, "There is no *law music* in heaven: there all their song is 'Worthy is the Lamb.' " The blood of ransom has atoned for *all sin.*

A Calloused Heart

Believers of a former age used to observe with thankfulness the occasions on which they were enabled to show "a kindly, penitential mourning for sin." At other times they would lament their deadness. Yet it never occurred to them that the coldness of their affections should cause them to restrain from prayer before God. On the contrary, they were of one mind with "a laborious and successful wrestler at the throne of grace," who determined that "he would never give up enumerating and confessing his sins until his heart was melted in contrition and penitential sorrow." There may be many explanations for such deadness of heart.

He who was once like a flame of fire in his Master's service may have allowed the fervor of his first love to decline for want of fuel, or the lack of watchful care, until only a little heap of gray ashes smoldered on the altar of his affections. His greatest sorrow is that he has no sorrow for sin; his heaviest burden is that he is unburdened. "Oh, that I were once again under the terrors of Christ" was the cry of one who had hung in agony over the brink of the pit. Suspended there, he had learned that a cold heart toward Christ was insufferable. Those who are in such a state are often nearer the Savior than they know. Shepard of New England, speaking from a wide experience, says, "More are drawn to Christ under the sense of a dead, blind heart than by all sorrows, humiliations, and terrors."

That which impresses us as deadness of heart may be the operation of the Holy Spirit, convincing us of sins that have gone unnoticed. As one looks at a far distant galaxy and sees it only as a wreath of dimming mist, so one becomes conscious of innumerable unregarded sins merely by the shadow that they fling upon the face of the heavens. But when one observes the nebulous drift through a telescope, it resolves itself into a cluster of stars, almost infinite in number. When one examines, in the secret place of communion, the cloud that darkens the face of God, it is seen to scatter and break into a multitude of sins. If then, in the hour of prayer we have no living communion with God, let us plead with the psalmist, "Search me, O God, and know my heart; test me and know my anxious thoughts. See if there is any offensive way in me, and lead me in the way everlasting" (Psalm 139:23–24). He who has engaged to "search Jerusalem with candles" (Zephaniah 1:12, KJV) will examine us through and through. He will test us like the way silver is authenticated, and will sift us like wheat. He will bring up from the unexplored depths of our nature all that is contrary to the mind of Christ, and will reduce every thought and imagination to the obedience of His will.

Deadness of heart may arise from the consciousness of our multitudinous sins of omission—duties unattempted, opportunities unimproved, grace disregarded. Often, when we kneel in prayer, "the lost years cry out" behind us. What was told of Archbishop Ussher might be said of many of the Lord's servants, "He prayed often and with great humility that God would forgive him his sins of omission and his failing in his duty" Each day is a vessel to be freighted with holy deeds and earnest endeavors before it weighs anchor and sets sail for the eternal shores. How many hours we mis-spend! How many occasions we lose! How many precious gifts of God we squander! Meanwhile the world passes away, and the fashion of it fades.

There is that that lies deeper in the soul than even secret sin—there is native sinfulness, the body of death. When we acknowledge the depravity of our nature we should endeavor to speak according to the measure of our experience. We can scarcely exaggerate the facts, but we may easily overstate our appreciation of them. As we advance in grace, as we become accustomed to holding our lightest thought of feeling within the piercing illumination of the divine purity, as we open the most hidden recesses of our being to the gracious influences of the good Spirit of God, we are led into a greater understanding of the sinfulness of inbred sin. Then we lament with Ezra, "O my God, I am too ashamed and disgraced to lift up my face to you, my God" (Ezra 9:6). It is reported of Luther that for one long day his inborn sinfulness revealed itself in dreadful manifestations so vehement and terrifying that "the very venom of them drank up his spirits, and his body seemed dead—neither speech, sense, blood, nor heat appeared in him."

On a day of special fasting and prayer Thomas Shepard of Cambridge, Connecticut, wrote as follows: "November 3rd. I saw sin as my greatest evil and that I was vile, but God was good only, whom my sins did cross. I saw what cause I had to loathe myself. . . . The Lord also gave me some glimpse of myself. It was a good day and time for me. . . . I went to God, and rested on Him. . . . I began to consider whether all the country did not fare the worse for my sins.

I saw that it was so, and this was a humbling thought to me."

Jonathan Edwards had at one time an amazing discovery of the beauty and glory of Christ. After recording it in his diary, he continued, "My wickedness, as I am in myself, has long appeared to me perfectly indescribable, and swallowing up all thought and imagination like an infinite deluge or mountains over my head. I know not how to express better what my sins appear to me to be than by heaping infinite upon infinite, and multiplying infinite by infinite. Very often for these many years these expressions are in my mind and in my mouth, 'Infinite upon infinite! Infinite upon infinite!' "

When Dr. John Duncan was drawing near to death, he remarked with great earnestness, "I am thinking with horror of the carnal mind, enmity against God; I never get a sight of it but it produces horror, even bodily sickness."

These are solemn experiences. Perhaps God leads few of His children through waters so wild and deep. Nor must we try to follow unless He points the way. Above all, we dare not in confessions that are addressed to a holy God simulate an experience that we have never known. Instead, let us, as far as God has revealed it to us, confess the deep sin of our nature. Dr. Payson said, with much truth, that the only "sign of one's being in Christ that Satan cannot counterfeit" is the grief and sorrow that true believers undergo when God discloses to them the sinfulness of inbred sin.

On the other hand, the love of Christ at times so fills the heart that though the remembrance of sin continues, the sense of sin is lost. It is swallowed up in a measureless ocean of peace and grace. Such high moments of visitation from the living God are surely a prelude to the joy of heaven. For the song of the redeemed in glory is unlike the praises of earth, because while it also celebrates the death of the Lamb of God there is in it no mention of sin. All the poisonous fruits of our iniquity have been killed. All the bitter consequences of our evil deeds have been blotted out. The only relics of sin that are found in heaven are the scarred feet and hands and side of the Redeemer. So when the saved from earth recall their former transgression they look to Christ. The remembrance of sin dies in the love of Him who wore the crown of thorns and endured the cross.

The fouler was the error,
  The sadder was the fall,
The ampler are the praises
  Of Him who pardoned all.

Make me sensible of real answers to actual requests, as evidence of an interchange between myself on earth and my Savior in heaven.

—*Thomas Chalmers*

O brother, pray; in spite of Satan, pray; spend hours in prayer; rather neglect friends than not pray; rather fast, and lose breakfast, dinner, tea, and supper—and sleep, too—than not pray. And we must not talk about prayer; we must pray in right earnest. The Lord is near. He comes softly while the virgins slumber.

—*A. A. Bonar*

The main lesson about prayer is just this: Do it! Do it! Do it! You want to be taught to pray. My answer is: pray and never faint, and then you shall never fail. There is no peradventure. You cannot fail. . . . A sense of real want is at the very root of prayer.

—*John Laidlaw*

6

The Engagement: Request

Once when the late Dr. Moody Stuart happened to be in Huntly, Duncan Matheson took him to see some earnest Christian people. He visited, among others, an aged woman who was in her own way a "character." Before leaving, he prayed with her. She, as was her habit, emphasized each petition with some ejaculatory comment, or note of assent. Toward the close of his prayer, he asked that God, according to His promise, would give her "all things." The old lady interjected, "All things? Now, that *would* be a lift."

The mingling of comfort and dubiety revealed by that quaint interpolation is characteristic of the faith of very many of the children of God when they are brought face-to-face with some great promise addressed to believing prayer. "If you believe, you will receive whatever you ask for in prayer" (Matthew 21:22); "I tell you, whatever you ask for in prayer, believe that you have received it, and it will be yours" (Mark 11:24); "If you remain in me and my words remain in you, ask whatever you wish, and it will be given you" (John 15:7). It is so reasonable to think that He who did not spare His own Son should also freely give us all things, and yet it is so hard to believe that He will. As Dr. Moody Stuart says elsewhere, the controversy is between the mustard seed and the mountain. "The trial is whether the mountain shall bury the mustard seed, or the mustard seed so small, and the mountain so great, that faith is not easily come by." Indeed, it is literally "the gift of God." It is a divinely implanted persuasion, the fruit of much spiritual instruction and discipline. It is vision in a clearer light than that of earth.

Elements of Faith

The prayer of faith, like some plant rooted in a fruitful soil, draws its virtue from a disposition that has been brought into conformity with the mind of Christ.

1. It is subject to the divine will—"This is the assurance we have in approaching God: that if we ask anything according to his will, he hears us" (1 John 5:14).

2. It is restrained within the interest of Christ—"And I will do whatever you ask in my name, so that the Son may bring glory to the Father" (John 14:13).

3. It is instructed in the truth—"If you remain in me and my words remain in you, ask whatever you wish, and it will be given you" (John 15:7).

4. It is energized by the Spirit—"Now to him who is able to do immeasurably more than all we ask or imagine, according to his power that is at work within us" (Ephesians 3:20).

5. It is interwoven with love and mercy—"And when you stand praying, if you hold anything against anyone, forgive him, so that your Father in heaven may forgive you your sins" (Mark 11:25).

6. It is accompanied with obedience—"We have confidence before God and receive from him anything we ask,

because we obey his commands and do what pleases him" (1 John 3:21–22).

7. It is so earnest that it will not accept denial—"Ask and it will be given to you; seek and you will find; knock and the door will be opened to you" (Luke 11:9).

8. It goes out to look for and to hasten its answer—"The prayer of a righteous man is powerful and effective" (James 5:16).

Sibbes wrote that "in prayer we tempt God if we ask for that which we labor not. Our faithful endeavors must second our devotion. . . . If we pray for grace and neglect the spring from which it comes, how can we succeed? It was a rule in ancient times that said, 'Lay thy hand to the plough, and then pray.' No man should pray without ploughing, nor plough without prayer."

Although the prayer of faith springs from a divinely implanted disposition, there is nothing mysterious in the act of faith. It is simply an assurance that relies upon a sufficient warning. In the first instance, the authority of faith is the Word of God. The promises of God are letters of credit, drawn on the bank of heaven, to be honored on sight. Some time ago a bundle of Bank of England notes was stolen, but they were unsigned, and therefore worthless. But the promises of God are all witnessed to by the eternal truth, and are countersigned in the blood of the cross. They are subject to no discount and those who present them will receive their full face value. "I am the Lord; I will speak, and the word that I shall speak shall be performed."

The Word of God rests on the divine character. Therefore we are taught to pray, "O Lord . . . do it, for your name's sake." God is our Father, and He knows what things we have need of. He is our God in covenant—our own God—and He will bless us. He is the God and Father of our Lord Jesus Christ, and He will secure to His well-beloved Son the inheritance that He has purchased in blood. He is the source of blessing, from whom the Comforter proceeds, and the prayer that He inspires He will fulfill.

In the intercession of Daniel the prophet we have a signal illustration of petitions founded on this twofold authority. "[He] understood from the Scriptures, according to the word of the Lord given to Jeremiah the prophet, that the desolation of Jerusalem would last seventy years" (Daniel 9:2). But the prophet does not place his trust only on the promise, he appeals to that which is due according to the divine character. "Now, our God, hear the prayers and petitions of your servant. For your sake, O Lord, look with favor on your desolate sanctuary. Give ear, O God, and hear; open your eyes and see the desolation of the city that bears your name. We do not make requests of you because we are righteous, but because of your great mercy. O Lord, listen! O Lord, forgive! O Lord, hear and act! For your sake, O my God, do not delay, because your city and your people bear your name" (Daniel 9:17–19).

It may be objected that if our Father knows what things we have need of before we ask Him, and if it is His good pleasure to give us the kingdom, is it necessary that we should present our petitions deliberately before Him? The simplest answer to that question is that we are instructed to do so. In the Old Testament we read, "This is what the Sovereign LORD says: Once again I will yield to the plea of the house of Israel and do this for them" (Ezekiel 36:37), and in the New Testament, "In everything, by prayer and petition, with thanksgiving, present your requests to God" (Philippians 4:6).

We have a striking example of the working of this divine law in the case of Elijah. He had preserved unhesitating fidelity toward God, and so had fulfilled the conditions by which fellowship with the Holy One is secured and maintained: "As the Lord God of Israel liveth, before whom I stand, there shall not be dew nor rain these years, but according to my word" (1 Kings 17:1, KJV). He had won Israel back to covenant allegiance: "When all the people saw this, they fell prostrate and cried, 'The Lord—he is God! The Lord—he is God!' " (1 Kings 18:39). He had received and acted upon a definite promise, "Elijah said to Ahab, 'Go, eat and drink, for there is the sound of a heavy rain' " (1 Kings 18:41). He had the inward assurance that God's answer to his long, insistent and repeated prayer was already on its way—"for there is the sound of a heavy rain." Nevertheless, he did not cease from praying—he could not—until the skies grew dark with the gathering storm.

Persistence

It is possible, however, to suggest certain reasons why we should energetically insist and repeatedly implore God for those blessings which are already ours in Christ.

Our continued and humble dependence on the grace of God is secured through prayer. If the gift of the covenant came to us without solicitation, as the gifts of nature do, we might be tempted to hold ourselves in independence of God. "You may say to yourself, 'My power and the strength of my hands have produced this wealth for me' "(Deuteronomy 8:17). Flavel said, "Prayer not only obtains mercies; it sweetens and sanctifies them" (*Works*, vol. 5, p. 351).

The Lord desires to have us often in communion with Him. Isaac Ambrose encourages us toward a proper focus in prayer. "We must draw away from prayer, from resting in it, or trusting upon it. A man may preach much, and instead of drawing closer to God, or enjoying sweet communion with Christ, he may draw closer to prayer, his thoughts more upon his prayer than upon God to whom he prays. He may live more upon his prayer cushion than upon Christ. When a man indeed draws closer to God in prayer, he forgets prayer, and remembers God. Prayer goes for nothing, but Christ is all" (*Prima Media et Ultima*, p. 332).

The reluctance of the carnal heart to dwell in God's presence is appalling. We would rather speak *of* Him than *to* Him. How often does He hear us saying, "Your companions listen to your voice; cause me to hear it"? A father will prize an ill-spelled, blotted scrawl from his little child because it is a pledge and seal of love. Gilmour of Mongolia bound into a small volume the brief childlike letters that had been sent to him by his sons. He carried these with him during his Mongolian wanderings, and whenever he looked at them he found unfailing solace and refreshment. The Lord considers the prayers of His saints to be precious in His sight.

A great deal must be accomplished in us before we are fit to use, in a worthy manner, the gifts we covet. God effects this preparation of heart largely by delaying to grant our request at once, thereby holding us in the truth of His presence until we are brought into a spiritual understanding of the will of Christ for us in this respect. Anselm of Canterbury expanded on this idea when he said, "God does not delay to hear our prayers because He has no mind to give, but that, by enlarging our desires, He may give us the more largely." If a friend, out of his way, comes to us hungry and seeks from our hands the bread of life, and we have nothing to set before him, we must go to Him who has the unending store of blessing. (See Luke 11:6.) If He answers, "Trouble me not," it is only that we may understand the nature of the blessing we seek, and be equipped to dispense the bounty of God correctly.

Once more, we are called to be fellow-laborers together with God in prayer, as in all other ministries. The exalted Savior ever lives to make intercession. To His redeemed people He says, "Stay here and keep watch with me" (Matthew 26:38). There is a great work to be done in the hearts of men and there is a fierce battle to be waged with spiritual wickedness in heavenly places. Demons are to be cast out, the potencies of hell to be restrained, and the works of the devil to be destroyed. In these things it is by prayer above all other means that we shall be able to cooperate with the Captain of the Lord's host.

A. J. Gordon, in his book *The Holy Spirit in Missions*, tells of the need for believers to persevere and wait on the Lord. "It was seven years before Carey baptized his first convert in India. It was seven years before Judson won his first disciple in Burma. Morrison toiled seven years before the first Chinese were brought to Christ. Moffat declared that he waited seven years to see the first evident moving of the Holy Spirit upon his Bechuanas of Africa. Henry Richards labored seven years on the Congo before the first convert was gained at Banza Manteka."

> God spake, and gave us the word to keep;
> Bade never fold the hands, nor sleep
> 'Mid a faithless world—at watch and ward
> Till Christ at the end relieve our guard.
> By His servant Moses the watch was set;
> Though near upon cockcrow we keep it yet.

When prayer rises to its true level, self with its concerns and needs is for the time forgotten, and the interests of Christ fill and sometimes overwhelm the soul. It is then that prayer becomes most urgent and intense. It was said of Luther that he prayed "with as much reverence as if he were praying to God, and with as much boldness as if he had been speaking to a friend." One remarked of the prayers of Guthrie of Fenwick that "every word would fill a firlot [a measure of corn]." Livingstone reports of Robert Bruce that in prayer "every sentence was like a strong bolt shot up to heaven." The biographer of Richard Baxter tells us that when he gathered his spirit together to pray, it "took wing for heaven." It is related in similar terms of Archbishop Leighton that "his manner of praying was so earnest and persistent that his soul mounted up to God in the flame of his own aspirations." Henry Martyn notes in his diary that having set apart a day for fasting and humiliation, he began to pray for the establishment of the divine kingdom upon earth, with particular mention of India. He received an incredible amplification of energy and delight in prayer, such that he had never experienced before. He adds, "My whole soul wrestled with God. I knew not how to leave off crying to Him to fulfill His promises, chiefly pleading His own glorious power."

How much of the regeneration of central Africa do we not owe to the prayers of David Livingstone? He did not live to see the healing of "the open sore." It was not given to him to know the advancing Christian culture of "the dark continent." But the record of his prayers is on high. His journals give some slight indication of his lonely vigils, his daily and nightly intercessions. He lived praying for Africa. When he felt the coldness of death seizing upon his frame, he crept out of bed, and as he knelt upon the floor of the rude grass hut in Chitambo's village in Ilala, his soul took flight to God in prayer. He died, his sympathetic biographer informs us, "in the act of praying; prayer offered in that reverential attitude about which he was always so particular. He committed his own spirit, with all his dear ones, as was his desire, into the hands of his Savior. He committed Africa, his own dear Africa, with all her woes, sins and wrongs, to the Avenger of the oppressed, and the Redeemer of the lost."

Prayer is the means by which we obtain all the graces that rain down upon us from the divine Fountain of Goodness and Love.

—Laurence Scupoli

There was a poor widow woman in the countryside, as I came through, that was worth many of you. She was asked how she did in this evil time. "I do very well," she said. "I get more of one verse of the Bible now than I did of all the Bible in times past. He hath cast me the keys to the pantry door, and bidden me take my fill."

—Alexander Peden

The consolation of Scriptures consisteth in this, that reading in them the promises of God, we do anew confirm and fortify ourselves in hope; there falling unto us that which falls to one to whom the Lord promiseth by his Letters a thousand "duckets of income," who maintains himself in the hope to have that revenue through patience, fortifying his heart more and more through hope, when it seems to him that the accomplishment of the promise is delayed, no wise departing from his hope, and comforting himself with the Letter of the Lord.

—Juan de Valés (Nicholas Ferrar's translation)

7

The Hidden Riches of the Secret Place

The return of prayer is, in the first instance, personal and private. It is "riches stored in secret places" (Isaiah 45:3). As it passes out into life and action, it is made manifest. The Father who is in secret and who sees in secret rewards His servants "openly" (Matthew 6:6, KJV).

We read that when the Pilgrims had come almost to the end of the enchanted ground, "they perceived that a little before them was a solemn noise, as of one that was much concerned. So they went on, and looked before them; and, behold, they saw, as they thought, a man upon his knees with his hands and eyes lifted up, and speaking, as they thought, earnestly to one that was above. They drew nigh, but could not tell what he said; so they went softly till he was done. When he was done, he got up, and began to run toward the Celestial City."

This is the first reward of the secret place; through prayer our gifts come to life, and holiness is brought about in us. "Holiness," says Hewitson, "is a habit of mind. A setting of the Lord continually before one's eyes. A constant walking with God as one with whom we are agreed." In the attainment and maintenance of unbroken communion, "Prayer is among duties as faith is among graces." Richard Sibbes reminds us that "prayer exercises all the graces of the Spirit." Flavel confirmed this thought when he wrote, "You must strive to excel in this, because no grace within or service without can thrive without it." The excellent Berridge affirms that "all decays begin in the closet. No heart thrives without much secret conversation with God, and nothing will make amends for the lack of it." On the other hand, he acknowledges, "I never rose from secret prayer without some quickening. Even when I set about it with heaviness or reluctance, the Lord is pleased in mercy to meet me in it." Similarly, Fraser of Brea declares, "I find myself better or worse as I increase in prayer or delay in it."

If prayer is hindered, even though it be hindered by devotion to other duties of religion, the health of the soul is impaired. Henry Martyn laments in his diary that "want of private devotional reading and shortness of prayer, through incessant sermon-making, had produced much strangeness" between God and his soul. Communion with God is the condition of spiritual growth. It is the soil in which all the graces of the divine life root themselves. If the virtues were the work of man, we might perfect them one by one, but they are "the fruit of the Spirit," and grow together in one common life. When Philip Saphir embraced Christianity, he said, "I have found a religion for my whole nature." Holiness is the harmonious perfection, the "wholeness" of the soul.

While we abide in Christ we should not allow ourselves to be discouraged by the apparent slowness of our advancement in grace. In nature, growth proceeds with varying speed. Sibbes compares the progressive sanctification of believers to the increase in "herbs and trees," which "grow at the root in winter, in the leaf in summer, and in the seed in autumn." The first of these forms of increase seems very slow, the second is more rapid, and the third rushes on to full maturity. In a few days of early autumn a field of grain will seem to ripen more than in weeks of midsummer.

Communion with God discovers the excellence of His character, and by beholding Him the soul is transformed. Holiness is conformity to Christ, and this is secured by a growing intimacy with Him. It is evident that this consideration opens up a vast field for reflection. We shall merely indicate one or two of the many directions in which it applies.

First, the habit of prayerfulness produces a singular serenity of spirit. To use Bengel's phrase, we are "built up into a recollected consciousness of God." When one looks into the quiet eyes of Him that sits upon the throne, the tremors of the spirit are stilled. Pharaoh, king of Egypt, is but a noise, and the valley of the shadow of death is tuneful with songs of praise. Storms may rage beneath our feet, but the sky above is blue. We take our station with Christ in heavenly places, and we dwell in the Sabbath of God. "Here I lie," said Thomas Halyburton when his death hour was drawing near, "pained without pain, without strength yet strong." Seguier, a French Protestant, who was sentenced to death, was mockingly asked by one of his guards how he felt. He replied, "My soul is as a garden, full of shelter and fountains." There are towns in Europe that would be insufferably hot in midsummer were it not that rivers, issuing from the ice field of Switzerland, diffuse a cool and refreshing air even in the sultry noon. In the same way the river of the water of life, which flows from under the throne of God and the Lamb, makes glad the city of God.

"Prayer is the peace of our spirits, the stillness of our thoughts, the evenness of our recollection, the seat of our meditation, the rest of our cares, and the calm of our tempest" (Jeremy Taylor, *The Return of Prayers*). This applies also on a lower level. George Müller wrote in his *Autobiography*, "These last three days I have had very little real communion with God, and have therefore been very weak spiritually, and have several times felt irritability of temper. May God in mercy help me to have more secret prayer."

Secondly, those who continually exercise themselves in prayer are taught to rule their lives according to the will of God. This effect follows naturally upon the former, for "all noble, moral energy roots itself in moral calm."

Prayer is the acknowledgment of our creature-dependence. For the believer also it is the acknowledgment that he is not his own, but is, by reason of the great atonement, the "purchased possession" of the Son of God. Pope Pius IV, hearing of Calvin's death, exclaimed, "Ah, the strength of that proud heretic lay in this, that riches and honor were nothing to him." David Livingstone, in the heart of darkest Africa, wrote in his journal, "My Jesus, my King, my Life, my All, I again dedicate my whole self to Thee." Bengel spoke in the name of all the children of faith when he said, "All I am, and have, both in principle and practice, is to be summed up in this one expression: 'The Lord's property.' My belonging totally to Christ as my Savior is all my salvation and all my desire. I have no other glory than this, and I want no other." Afterward, when death drew near, the following words were pronounced over him. "Lord Jesus, to Thee I live, to Thee I suffer, to Thee I die. Thine I am in death and in life; save and bless me, O Savior, for ever and ever. Amen." At the words "Thine I am," he laid his right hand upon his heart, in token of his full and hearty assent, and so he fell asleep in Jesus. Such is the normal attitude of the redeemed soul, an attitude that prayer acknowledges and confirms.

In prayer we present ourselves to God, holding our motives in His clear light, and estimating them after the counsel of His will. Thus our thoughts and feelings stratify themselves (as in the process of levigation). Those that rise toward the honor of God take precedence over those that drift downward toward the gratification of self. That is the way the great decisions of life are prepared. In prayer, Jacob became Israel; in prayer, Daniel saw Christ's day and was glad; in prayer, Saul of Tarsus received his commission to go among the Gentiles; in prayer, the Son of Man accomplished His obedience, and embraced His cross. It does not always happen, however, that the cardinal points of life are recognized in the very place and hour of prayer.

Helmholtz, the celebrated physicist, used to say that his greatest discoveries came to him, not in the laboratory, but when he was walking along a country road, in perfect freedom of mind. Although his discoveries merely registered themselves then, they were really brought up to the birth in the laboratory. Whether it be in the place of prayer, or elsewhere, that life's great decisions frame themselves, undoubtedly it is in the silent hour that characters are molded and careers determined.

In his *Autobiography*, George Müller gives a striking testimony. "I never remember, in all my Christian course, a period now (March 1895) of sixty-nine years and four months, that I ever *sincerely* and *patiently* sought to know the will of God by the teaching of the Holy Ghost, through the instrumentality of the Word of God, but I have been *always* directed rightly. But if honesty of heart and uprightness before God were lacking, or if I did not patiently wait before God for instruction, or if I preferred the counsel of my fellowmen to the declarations of the Word of the living God, I made great mistakes."

As we present ourselves before the Lord in prayer, we open our hearts to the Holy Spirit—we yield to the inward impulse, and the divine energy commands our being. Our plans, if we have formed them at the dictation of nature, are laid aside, and the purpose of God in relation to our lives is accepted. As we are Spirit-born, let us be Spirit-controlled. "If we live in the Spirit, let us also walk in the Spirit" (Gal. 5:25, KJV).

Lastly, it is through the acceptance of the will of God for us that we are led out into a richer influence and a wider usefulness.

Montalembert once complained to Lacordaire, "How little it is that man can do for his fellows! Of all his miseries this is the greatest." It is true that we can effect little for one another by ordinary human means, but much may be done by prayer—

> More things are wrought by prayer
> Than this world dreams of.

Prayer brings the divine omnipotence into the occasions of life. We ask, and receive; and our joy is full.

An English scholar has told us that those who have helped him most were not learned divines nor eloquent preachers, but holy men and women who walked with God and who revealed unconsciously the unadorned goodness that the blessed Spirit had wrought in them. Those saintly persons had looked on Christ until they were changed into His likeness. They had tarried on the Mount of God until the uncreated glory shone upon their brows. Tradition affirms that Columbia, the Celtic missionary; Ruysbroek, the recluse of Groenendaal; John Welsh of Ayr, and many others, were wrapped in a soft and tempered radiance as they prayed. Such legends, no doubt, were created by the remembrance of lives that had been transfigured.

> I saw a Saint. How canst thou tell that he
> Thou sawest was a Saint?

I saw one like to Christ, so luminously
    By patient deeds of love, his mortal taint
Seemed made his groundwork for humility.

A changed life is not the only gift that God bestows upon us when we stand in the unseen Presence. When Moses came from the Mount, he was as it were transfigured in the eyes of the children of Israel. He also bore in his hands the tables of testimony—the pledges of that covenant, ordered and sure, which had been sealed to him for them. His prayer had saved the people of election, and the law tablets were the sign. John Nelson, hearing someone unfavorably comparing John Wesley with a pulpit celebrity of the time, replied, "But *he* has not tarried in the Upper Room as John Wesley has done." It is this tarrying in the Upper Room that secures the endowment of power.

Jesus, Lord God from all eternity,
Whom love of us brought down to shame,
I plead Thy life with Thee,
I plead Thy death, I plead Thy name.
Jesus, Lord God of every living soul,
Thy love exceeds its uttered fame,
Thy will can make us whole.
I plead Thyself, I plead Thy name.

—*Christina Rossetti*

None can believe how powerful prayer is, and what it is able to effect, but those who have learned it by experience. It is a great matter when in extreme need to take hold on prayer. I know whenever I have prayed earnestly that I have been amply heard, and have obtained more than I prayed for. God indeed sometimes delayed, but at last He came.

—*Luther*

8

The Public Reward

I sought Him in my hour of need;
(Lord God now hear my prayer!)
For death He gave me life indeed,
And comfort for despair.
For this my thanks shall endless be,
Oh thank Him, thank Him now with me,
Give to our God the glory!

—J. J. Schutz

In their anxiety to magnify the personal benefits that are derived from communion with God, the Greek fathers used to employ the figure of a boat moored to a ship. If one were to draw upon the rope, they said, the ship would remain unmoved, but the boat would at once respond to the pull. Apparently they forgot, or did not know, that in mechanics "action and reaction are equal and opposite." The larger vessel receives as much of an effect as the smaller, but the greater bulk of the ship makes the displacement much less obvious. In prayer also, the influence is reciprocal. There is, as we have seen, a heightened exercise of all the Christian graces, but there are also direct answers to petitions offered in faith.

If we do not expect to receive answers to our requests, our whole conception of prayer is at fault. "None ask in earnest," says Trail, "but they test their success. There is no surer and plainer mark of trifling in prayer than when men are careless with what they get by prayer." To the same effect Richard Sibbes writes, "We should watch daily, continue instant in prayer, strengthen our supplications with arguments from God's Word and promises, and mark how our prayers succeed. When we shoot an arrow we look to its fall; when we send a ship to sea we look for its return; and when we sow we look for a harvest. . . . It is atheism—to pray and not to wait in hope. A sincere Christian will pray, wait, strengthen his heart with the promises, and never leave praying and looking up till God gives him a gracious answer."

If the answer is delayed, we ought to ask ourselves if that that we desire is truly according to the will of God. If we are satisfied that it is, we ought to continue "instant in prayer." Bengel gives his judgment that "a Christian should not leave off praying till his heavenly Father gives him leave by permitting him to obtain something." George Müller drew encouragement from the fact that he had been enabled to persevere in prayer daily, during twenty-nine years, for a certain spiritual blessing long withheld. "At home and abroad, in this country and in foreign lands, in health and in sickness, however much occupied, I have been enabled day by day by God's help to bring this matter before Him, and still I have not the full answer. Nevertheless, I look for it. I expect it confidently. The very fact that day after day, and year after year, for twenty-nine years, the Lord has enabled me to continue patiently, believingly, to wait on Him for the blessing, still further encourages me to wait on. So fully am I assured that God hears me about this matter that I have often been enabled to praise Him beforehand for the full answer, which I shall ultimately receive to my prayers on this subject." On this point Müller says elsewhere, "It is not enough to begin to pray, nor to pray properly, nor is it enough to continue for a time to pray, but we must patiently, believingly, continue in prayer until we obtain an answer. Furthermore, we have not only to continue in prayer until the end, but we have also to believe that God does hear us and will answer our prayers. Most frequently we fail in not continuing in prayer until the blessing is obtained, and in not expecting the blessing."

We should not doubt that those prayers that are according to the will of God shall have a full answer, because with regard to them we rest our confidence on the Word and Name of Christ. Full assurance to many of our requests does not come easily. They do not clearly stand in the divine will, so do not yield certainty to us. With regard to many of them our prayers seem to return empty.

Moses desired to pass over Jordan with the tribes, but Jehovah said to him, "Do not speak to me anymore about this matter" (Deuteronomy 3:26). Paul asked the Lord three times that the thorn that rankled in his flesh might be withdrawn. The only response granted was "My grace is sufficient for you" (2 Corinthians 12:9). John the beloved disciple encourages us to pray for the salvation of our brethren. Yet even as we address ourselves to this holy duty, he reminds us that "there is a sin that leads to death" (1 John 5:16), in the face of which, apparently, prayer will not prevail.

Richard Sibbes, in his *Divine Meditations*, reminds us that we can indeed be sure that "whatsoever is good for God's children they shall have it, for all is theirs to help them toward heaven. Therefore, if poverty be good they shall have it, if disgrace or crosses be good they shall have them, for all is ours to promote our greatest prosperity."

When we pray for temporal blessings, we are sometimes conscious of the special aid of the Spirit of intercession. This is a reason to believe that our prayer is well-pleasing to God. We must be careful, however, not to confound the yearnings of nature with the promptings of the Spirit. Only those whose eye is single, and whose whole body, therefore, is full of light, can safely distinguish between the impulses of the flesh and of the Spirit. The following extract from the *Life of John Howe* may serve to point a caution that has sometimes been too lightly heeded:

"At that time [in the days of the English Commonwealth] an erroneous opinion, still cherished by some pious people, concerning the effectiveness of a special faith in prayer, pervaded the religious community. The idea was entertained that if a believer was led to seek a favor in prayer, such as the recovery or conversion of a child, or victory on the battlefield, with unusual fervor, and with the strong persuasion that the prayer would be favorably answered, it would certainly come to pass. This notion was carried by some to still greater lengths of extravagance, until it amounted to a virtual assertion of inspiration. The court of Cromwell was a fertile soil for the nourishment of a conceit like this; indeed, it appears to have taken deep hold of the mind of the Protector himself. Thoroughly convinced of its erroneous nature and unhallowed tendencies, and having listened to a sermon at Whitehall that was designed to maintain and defend it, Howe felt himself bound in conscience to expose its absurdity when next he should preach before Cromwell. This he did. . . . Cromwell's brow furnished indications of his displeasure during the delivery of the discourse, and a certain coolness in his manner afterward, but the matter was never mentioned between them."

Subject to this caution we may very often derive encouragement from the fervor of our petitions. John Livingstone made this note in his private papers: "After prayer, I am to look back and recapitulate what petitions God has put in my mouth. These I am to count as blessings promised and to look for their performance." Augustus Toplady speaks with even less reserve: "I can, to the best of my remembrance and belief, truly say that I never yet have had one promise or assurance concerning temporal things, impressed upon me beforehand by way of communion with God, which the event did not realize. I never, that I know of, knew it to fail in any one single instance." This "particular faith in prayer" sometimes engages itself in apprehending the answer to prayers offered for spiritual interests. A memorable revival occurred in Kilsyth, of which the firstfruits were seen on Tuesday, July 23, 1839.

William Burns, writing about that time, said, "I have since heard that some of the people of God in Kilsyth had been longing and wrestling for a time of refreshing from the Lord's presence. During much of the previous night, after travailing in birth for souls, came to the meeting not only with the hope, but with the certain anticipation of God's glorious appearing. This came from the impressions they had received upon their own souls of Jehovah's approaching glory and majesty."

What things would form the burden of our request? Maximus of Tyre declared that he would not ask the gods for anything but goodness, peace, and hope in death. But we Christians may ask our Father for all that we need. Only let our desires be restrained, and our prayers unselfish. The personal petitions contained in the Lord's Prayer are very modest—daily bread, forgiveness, and deliverance from sin's power. Yet these comprise all things that pertain to life and godliness.

Bread and water, and a place of shelter among the munitions of rocks, are assured to us. Garrison, and garrison fare! John Duncan, in his book *The Pulpit and Communion Table*, told this story: "Being asked by a lady if he would have bread and a glass of wine, he replied, 'If you please, I'll have bread and a glass of water.' 'Prison fare,' remarked the lady. 'No, garrison fare: He shall dwell on high; his place of defense *shall* be the munitions of rocks: bread shall be given him; his waters *shall be* sure' " (Isaiah 33:16, KJV). We are not often reduced to such simplicity of supply; God is so much better than His word. He feeds us with food convenient, and if He ever should permit us to hunger, it is only that our spiritual nature may be enriched.

Man does not live by bread alone. Health and comfort, the joys of home, and the pleasures of knowledge are blessings for which we may rightfully ask. They will not be withheld unless our Father judges it best that we should be deprived of them. If He should bar our repeated request, and refuse to receive our prayer, we must then reply with the Firstborn among many, " 'Abba, Father,' . . . everything is possible for you. . . . Yet not what I will, but what you will" (Mark 14:36). Dwight L. Moody used to say that he thanked God with all his heart that many of his most earnest prayers had not been granted. When we reach the end of our journey, if not before, we shall be able to say, "Not one word has failed of all the good promises he gave" (1 Kings 8:56).

When we pray for spiritual blessings we shall never ask in vain. James Gilmour wrote to one who asked his counsel: "All I know about the process is just going to God and telling what I want, and asking to be allowed to have it. 'Seek, and ye shall find; ask, and ye shall receive.' I know no secret but this." And again, "You say you want reviving—go directly to Jesus and ask it straight out, and you'll get it straight away. This revived state is not a thing you need to work yourself up into, or need others to help you to rise into, or need to come to England to have operated upon you. Jesus can effect it anywhere, and does effect it everywhere, whenever a man or woman, or men and women, ask for it. 'Ask, and ye shall receive.' My dear brother, I have learned that the source of much blessing is just to go to Jesus, and tell Him what you need."

A Scottish covenanter reports that he received a greater increase of grace in one afternoon spent in prayer than during a year before. After two days of prayer in the woods of Anwoth, Samuel Rutherford received the white stone and a new name, to be "a graced minister of Jesus Christ." How many kneeling in an upper chamber have received the heavenly baptism into "a sense of all conditions," and the witness of the tongue of fire? All the storehouses of God open at the voice of faith.

Examples of Answered Prayer

It is probable that answers to prayer will always bring their own token to the supplicant, but he may not always be able to convince others that the events that happened are due to the direct interposition of God. Let us take two examples chosen almost at random.

"A Christian friend once sprang after his boy, who had fallen into the swollen flood of the Wupper. As he dove in he cried, 'Lord, teach me to swim!' He swam skillfully, though he had never tried it before, and saved his child" (F. W. Krummacher, *Autobiography*, Edinburgh, 1869, p. 143).

"Once when a sudden and terrific hailstorm was pouring down upon the fields, and likely to occasion serious damage, a person rushed into Bengel's room and exclaimed, 'Alas, sir, everything will be destroyed; we shall lose all!' Bengel, with composure, went to the window, opened it, lifted up his hands to heaven, and said, 'Father, restrain it,' and the tempest actually abated from that moment" (J.C.F. Burk, *Memoirs of J. A. Bengel*, London, 1837, pp. 491–492).

Often, however, the reward of prayer is so conspicuous that it is scarcely possible to ignore the connection between the petition and the answer. Let us take as an example of this the case of charitable institutions founded by their pious promoters on the promises of God.

The *Pietas Hallensis* is little else than an enumeration of deliverances granted to Dr. Francke in connection with the orphan houses at Halle. Here is one: "Another time I stood in need of a great sum of money, even a hundred crowns would not have served the turn, and yet I saw not the least appearance how I might be supplied with even a hundred groats. The steward came and set forth the want we were in. I bade him come again after dinner, and I resolved to put up my prayers to the Lord for His assistance. When he came in again after dinner, I was still in the same want, and so appointed him to come in the evening. In the meantime a friend of mine had come to see me, and with him I joined in prayers, and found myself much moved to praise and magnify the Lord for all His admirable dealings toward mankind, even from the beginning of the world, and the most remarkable instances came readily to my remembrance while I was praying. I was so elevated in praising and magnifying God that I insisted only on that exercise of my present devotion, and found no inclination to put up many anxious petitions to be delivered about the present necessity. At length my friend needed to take his leave so I accompanied him to the door, where I found the steward waiting on one side for the money he wanted, and on the other a person who brought a hundred and fifty crowns for the support of the hospital."

The history of George Müller's homes at Ashley Downs is written vividly on the conscience of christendom. Mr. Müller, among many trials to faith, encountered one which was especially sharp. Looking back to it in later years, he commemorates the Lord's deliverance, and adds, "The only inconvenience that we had in this case was that our dinner was about half an hour later than usual. Such a thing, as far as I remember, scarcely ever occurred before, and has never occurred since."

William Quarrier balanced the accounts of the homes at Bridge of Weir every month. If at any time it appeared probable that the balance would fall on the wrong side, he called his fellow workers to prayer, and invariably the needed funds came in. Almost at the close of his life, he testified that he had never been in debt one hour.

"The God that answereth by orphanages," exclaimed Charles H. Spurgeon, "let Him be God."

Less tangible, but no less obvious, are the answers granted to prayers for the extension of the Redeemer's kingdom upon earth. To illustrate this point suitably it would be necessary to write out the history of the whole church of Christ.

One could almost wish that this were the beginning and not the close of this volume. How the instances crowd upon the memory and stir the imagination!

By prayer a handful of "unlearned and ignorant men," hardhanded from the oar and the rudder, the mattock and the pruning hook, "turned the world upside down," and spread the name of Christ beyond the limits of the Roman power.

By prayer the tentmaker of Tarsus won the dissolute Corinthians to purity and faith. "A Church of God in Corinth . . . a blessed and astounding paradox!" He laid the enduring foundations of Western Christianity, and raised the name of Jesus high in the very palace of Nero.

The ruined cells on many barren islets in our Scottish seas remind us of the weeks and months of prayer and fasting by which the Celtic missionaries, in the space of one generation, won Caledonia for Christ.

The prayers of Luther and his co-workers sent the great

truths of the Gospel flying across Europe "as on the wings of angels."

The moorland and the mountains of Scotland are to this hour witnesses that "a fair meeting" between a covenanting Christ and a covenanted land were drawn on by the prayers of Welsh and Cargill, Guthrie and Blackadder, Peden and Cameron.

Before the great revival in Gallneukirchen broke out, Martin Boos spent hours and days, and often nights, in lonely agonies of intercession. Afterward, when he preached, his words were as flame, and the hearts of the people as grass.

A sermon preached in Clynnog, Caernarvonshire, by Robert Roberts was the apparent cause of a widespread awakening in Wales. It is said that a hundred persons were savingly impressed by its delivery. Some days later, a friend of the preacher, John Williams of Dolyddelen, said, "Tell me, Roberts, where did you get that wonderful sermon?" "Come here, John," said Roberts. He led him to a small parlor, and continued, "It was here I found that sermon you speak of—on the floor here, all night long, turning backward and forward, with my face sometimes on the earth."

Ah! it is always so. Those who have turned many to righteousness have labored early and late with the weapon called "all-prayer."

Joseph Alleine "was infinitely and insatiably greedy for the conversion of souls." It was told of him that "at the time of his health, he did rise constantly at or before four o'clock. . . . From four till eight he spent in prayer, holy contemplation, and singing of psalms, in which he much delighted. . . . Sometimes he would suspend the routine of parochial engagements and devote whole days to these secret exercises. Sometimes he would contrive to be alone in some void house, or else in some sequestered spot in the open valley.

It was said of William Grimshaw, the apostle of Yorkshire, that "it was his custom to rise early in the morning—at five in the winter, and at four in the summer—that he might begin the day with God."

George Whitefield frequently spent whole nights in meditation and prayer, and often rose from his bed in the night to intercede for perishing souls. He says, "Whole days and weeks have I spent prostrate on the ground in silent or vocal prayer."

The biographer of Payson observes that "prayer was preeminently the business of his life," He used to maintain that he pitied that Christian who could not enter into the meaning of the words, "groans that words cannot express" (Romans 8:26). It is related of him that he "wore the hard wood boards into grooves where his knees pressed so often and so long."

In a word, every gracious work that has been accomplished within the kingdom of God has been begun, fostered, and consummated by prayer. "What is the secret of this revival?" asked one in 1905 to Evan Roberts. "There is no secret," was the reply. "It is only, 'Ask, and receive.' "

Suggestions for Further Reading From Bethany House Publishers:

Alone With God —Campbell McAlpine
Answers to Prayer —Charles G. Finney
The Believer's Prayer Life —Andrew Murray
The Believer's Secret of Waiting on God —Andrew Murray
The Believer's School of Prayer —Andrew Murray
George Müller: Man of Faith and Miracles —Basil Miller
How to Have a Daily Quiet Time —Larry Christenson
John Hyde —Francis McGaw
The Ministry of Intercessory Prayer —Andrew Murray
Principles of Prayer —Charles G. Finney
Revival Praying —Leonard Ravenhill
The Secret of Believing Prayer —Andrew Murray
Seven Guides to Effective Prayer —Colin Whittaker
A Treasury of Prayer —E. M. Bounds